'A clear and methodical approach to negotiation, drawing upon the vast and unique professional experiences of Jim Houghton and Kirk Kinnell in the field. It provides an essential cornerstone for understanding the intricate dynamics of complex negotiation, blending strategic insight with psychological acumen and ethical considerations, offering readers a comprehensive and practical toolkit for navigating challenging negotiation scenarios with precision and principled conduct. A must-read for anyone engaged in difficult negotiation'

Claude Bruderlein, Negotiation Instructor, Harvard University

'I have been fortunate to work closely with Kirk for many years now. His skills as a negotiator are invaluable, just like his wisdom. This book is a part of himself. Enjoy!'

Marwan Mery, President, ADN Group

'A very compelling read'

Richard Mullender, The Listening Institute

'I am deeply inspired by Kirk's approach to negotiation, which he has developed as a former hostage and humanitarian negotiator'

Dr Thomas Leiber, inventor, engineer, entrepreneur

'Jim and Kirk have combined to produce a book that is both easy to read and yet full of ideas and recounted situations that stay with you, each bringing a sense of the urgency, discipline, energy and hard-won insight required to do what they excel at as seasoned professionals. Negotiation is often a fluid and stressed process that is very hard to capture within the covers of a book, but through combining their experiences of very different situations, Jim and Kirk have been as successful in that task as they have surely been in the day-to-day negotiating challenges that are the bedrock of their work'

Tim Birt, Partner, Osborne Clarke

'This is a book I should have read thirty years ago – it could have made life a lot easier!'

Peter Mead, Vice Chairman, Omnicom Group

Jim Houghton

For the past twenty years, Jim has been one of the foremost deal leads in the international marketing services industry. He's negotiated deals from every angle and in all the major international industry hubs, and is a partner at Waypoint Partners. Previously, as the European corporate development lead for the world's then largest and most acquisitive holding company, Omnicom Group, Jim delivered more than forty transactions. Seeing the value unintentionally being left on the table by both sides, Jim moved to M&A advisory and has successfully led transactions with buyers and sellers from across the globe, acting on both the sell side and buy side.

M&A in the marketing services industry offers the perfect storm of big businesses and private equity investors crashing together with passionate owner-managers in the pursuit of rapid international expansion and wealth. Big egos and high stakes make for intense and complex negotiations, and Jim has an enviable track record at finding paths that get these deals done.

Kirk Kinnell

Kirk brings the skills of hostage negotiation into the corporate world and everyday life. He joined the police in 1987 and worked in hostage negotiation for over two decades. In that time he was deployed on hundreds of hostage and crisis incidents, including as lead negotiator when UK nationals had been kidnapped overseas. He was made Head of Hostage Negotiation and Armed Policing in Scotland in 2015.

Kirk was also a leading member of the UK National Negotiator Group and Global International Negotiators Working Group. His global counter-terrorism strategy and training programme was adopted by the nations in the group and is still used today.

Kirk lectures on negotiation at universities and conferences all over the world, including Harvard Business School and the École des Hautes Études Commerciales de Paris (HEC). He has instructed at the Hostage Crisis Negotiator Course of the FBI, trained the Philippine National Police and delivers training to the private sector on corporate negotiations, listening and influencing skills, leadership and conflict resolution through his specialist consulting firm, Negotiated Resolutions.

THE WORK SMARTER GUIDE TO NEGOTIATION

Jim Houghton & Kirk Kinnell

Series Editor David Kean

A How To book

ROBINSON

ROBINSON

First published in Great Britain in 2024
by Robinson.

10 9 8 7 6 5 4 3 2 1

Copyright © Jim Houghton
and Kirk Kinnell, 2024

The moral right of the authors has been
asserted.

A CIP catalogue record for this book
is available from the British Library.

ISBN: 978-1-47214-881-0

Typeset in Sentinel and Scala Sans
by Ian Hughes.

Printed and bound in Great Britain by Clays
Ltd, Elcograf S.p.A.

Papers used by Robinson are from well-
managed forests and other responsible
sources.

MIX
Paper | Supporting
responsible forestry
FSC® C104740

Robinson
An imprint of
Little, Brown Book Group
Carmelite House
50 Victoria Embankment
London EC4Y 0DZ

An Hachette UK Company
www.hachette.co.uk

www.littlebrown.co.uk

How To Books are published by
Robinson, an imprint of Little, Brown
Book Group. We welcome proposals
from authors who have first-hand
experience of their subjects. Please set
out the aims of your book, its target
market and its suggested contents in an
email to howto@littlebrown.co.uk.

Authors' note

The professional and personal anecdotes in this book are all based on actual events. However, in order to protect those involved and to respect confidentiality, certain key details have been changed, including amalgamating events and characters where appropriate. Any similarity between these characters and real people is accidental. Dialogue exchanges are not verbatim, nor should they be treated as such.

Jim Houghton:

My dad – for the countless joyful games of 'name that advert' that really started my fascination with the world of advertising and brands that's given me so many rich and wonderful opportunities in life over the past three decades. To his collection of PG Tips memorabilia (especially Sargeant Chimp and Cyril the Cyclist) and his box of Bovril cubes with a commando dagger plunged through it.

Kirk Kinnell:

My wife Kirsteen and children Justine and Kirk who understood my sacrifice and its impact upon them. Richard Mullender and Marwan Mery, who both introduced and mentored me as I retired after thirty years of service and transitioned into the corporate world. They have also written incredible books on negotiation and encouraged me to take on that fresh challenge.

Contents

Introduction

Who relishes the prospect of negotiating? Most of us fear it. But, at home and at work, we find ourselves having to negotiate almost every single day of our lives. So much always seems to ride on every negotiation in life. From getting your toddler to go to bed at night, through getting a pay rise at work, to buying the house of your dreams.

If we're brutally honest, it's hard to think of anything more thankless or less appealing. Negotiating is a necessary evil – it only happens when you've failed to persuade someone else to do what you want them to do. Which means you're probably dealing with someone who's unhappy, upset or even angry. What happens if you screw it up? What if that person's important to you – just as important as the thing you can't agree about? What if the situation needs to be sorted out quickly because something or someone else vitally important depends on it?

It's stressful. And who truly enjoys that kind of stress?

Think of this book as *'stress inoculation training'*. The event in itself is not stressful; it is our inability to cope with it that makes it stressful. This book will give you that ability.

In negotiation we often feel that the balance of power is stacked against us. That feeling can be reduced considerably by training, practising and rehearsing *before* deployment in a live situation. Which is why we wrote this book: to show you how professionals approach negotiation and to help you be better prepared for whatever negotiation comes your way.

As full-time professional negotiators, we have our own philosophy on what negotiation is all about. As a police hostage negotiator, Kirk was trained by and worked with some of the best negotiators on the planet. People whose only goal was to help others out of situations when *they could not figure a way out on their own.*

As Kirk says:

> '*We engage people in many difficult circumstances without judgement, and never at any time did I feel that I was under extreme pressure. Nor did I ever think that I 'won' anything. Negotiation is not a win-lose option, as so many people think it is. Even the armed criminals who went to jail at the end of a siege still managed to get the best out of a potentially terrible deal.'*

Both of us share this philosophy: negotiation is not a zero-sum game with one winner and one loser. Real life is not like TV shows such as *The Apprentice* or *Succession*. Reading this book will not instantly empower you to crush your opponents. It is possible, desirable even, for every side to come out of the negotiation well. If you are clear on what you need from the negotiation – what your 'win' is – even if the other side is celebrating their own victory, you'll have something to celebrate too.

Negotiation is nuanced

We've done a lot of negotiating in our careers. This book tells our stories. It combines our experiences from dramatically different types of negotiations to offer you a series of practical, real-life examples on how to be prepared for and conduct whatever negotiation you might be facing. What holds true for keeping a hostage alive might hold the key to getting your toddler off to bed. Or for negotiating with your wedding caterer. Or agreeing a pay rise with your boss or a contract with a new client. And, for those in a real hurry, each story ends with a summary of the key negotiation lessons that are transferable to most environments.

There's a plethora of so-called experts who tell you how to negotiate. 'Circus conjurers', we call them – people who show you the tricks of the trade and promise the earth. We don't believe circus conjurers hold the answers. We have a healthy disregard for those who teach negotiation cynically, use psychology to trick people into agreement or promise crushing victory over your opponents. Negotiation is *not* the same as manipulation.

Manipulation is where we influence the behaviour of others for *personal gain*. Influence is something quite different. Influence is about provoking change for the benefit of *everyone* – with good intentions. We commence every negotiation with good and fair intentions for everyone involved.

We urge you to do the same.

All the concepts covered in this book have as their starting point good intentions and authenticity. When the party you are negotiating with recognises them as such, you will be met with a level of respect rather than mistrust and they will move your dialogue forward.

Trust is at the centre of this approach – that feeling of certainty that those with whom we are negotiating get it, that they see us as *reliable partners who find solutions that they can live with*. It may not make for good TV (which is not to say you won't find plenty of adrenaline-inducing stories in the book), but our approach works better in the real world, which is where you have to negotiate.

How to use this book

This book is for people who find themselves having to negotiate across a whole range of topics but who don't want to plough through a four-inch-thick theoretical textbook or who find an oversimplified list of negotiation platitudes unsatisfyingly superficial. It's written to reassure you that you're not alone. Negotiating can be stressful, intense and lonely. But you've got us with you now, and we're going to help make you a lot more resourceful, show you the right attitude and give you a versatile toolkit for approaching each situation you face.

Everything you will learn has been tested in extreme circumstances. Together they are a collection of skills that allow you to connect with people in a way that helps them see a situation from a different perspective and change their mind – which creates much better outcomes for you.

In this book you'll find twenty-two stories relating real-life negotiations we've conducted. Some are long, some short. Hopefully you'll never have to convince a gangster to surrender his sidearm or secure the release of colleagues taken hostage by guerrilla forces, but even if you don't, each story contains lessons that have universal applicability. You'll see the repeating themes and behavioural patterns that colour almost all negotiations, including the ones you have had or are yet to have.

We've organised the stories thematically into sections to help you navigate the main styles of negotiation situations. You'll see our philosophy running through each scenario and how it has shaped the process of the negotiation and its outcome. Dip into the stories individually or thematically. They're written to be accessible to you when you need help the most.

They aren't intended to tell you what to do; despite what some people say, there is no magic script you can follow to 'win' the deal, no one-size-fits-all approach. Instead, they'll allow you to draw parallels with your personal situation, prepare you for the twists and turns ahead and give you the courage to try new things – the things that have worked for us.

Right at the end of the book you will find a glossary of terms. Every now and again we have used technical terms which we use in our respective spheres of work – the glossary explains what they mean.

PART 1

The Key to any Negotiation: Empathy

Hostage negotiators have learned never to use the phrase, 'I understand'. Why? Because it is usually met by the other person shouting: 'how could you possibly understand?'.

Empathy is not:

- walking in the other person's shoes
- feeling their pain
- sympathising with them
- solving their problems

> *Empathy is the recognition and articulation of another's emotional state and their context.*

When we listen properly and when we get it right, we can reframe what we hear and see without being confrontational – to the point where we elicit the response:

- 'yes'
- 'exactly'
- 'you're right'

In that moment we move to an area of mutual agreement and understanding. *It is only when others feel heard and understood that they are open to anything we might say.* For the first time we are in agreement about something. Before that moment, we have been wasting our breath. We must free the emotional part of the brain before we can access the logical part, regardless of how long that takes.

So, negotiation is all about *context* and *empathy*. In almost every siege, suicide, hostage intervention or business negotiation we have conducted, empathy has been the key to unlocking a 'trapped mindset'. Usually the solution lies within the underlying unresolved emotions of the other person – this is often what is at the heart of the conflict.

CHAPTER 1

Start by opening up options, not closing them down

The outskirts of Glasgow. A man – let's call him Jack – had discharged a firearm from the upstairs window of a split-level flat. Armed police surrounded the block of flats, to contain the person involved and protect members of the public in the area.

Each officer took up a position around the outer perimeter of the block to observe the windows of the flat Jack was believed to be occupying. Once in place, the occupants of nearby houses were told to remain indoors and members of the public nearby were moved to a safe distance.

My brief was to engage Jack, the perpetrator, and attempt to negotiate his safe surrender. I was part of a four-person negotiation team. We decided on our strategy for engagement.

We tried to engage Jack in conversation. For the first few hours, he did not respond. We called him repeatedly on his mobile phone but he refused to pick up. But as others had seen movement inside the house, we knew that he was safe and well.

Eight long hours followed. We advertised our presence at his front door and texted reassuring messages to his mobile. We said that we were only trying to provide him with options that would be good for him. A relative of the man made us aware that he had taken some substances that would make him more difficult to reach for a little while.

In a situation like this, the primary need is for safety; safety for the public, safety for the neighbourhood, safety for our team and safety for the perpetrator. Which means you can never be in a hurry. We made no demands and our offer to talk was on the table for as long as necessary. As my working day drew to a close, our team had not yet opened any dialogue with the man. Our handover briefing to the team replacing us overnight was lengthy because we needed to ensure they understood the situation completely before we headed home.

When I checked in the following morning, I was informed that no progress had been made with Jack by the night-shift team. I drove straight to the location wondering how we would close this deal.

We were in a stalemate. We needed to do something to change the dynamic and build some trust between us and Jack. But given we knew he was armed, we had to proceed with extreme caution.

We needed a proper understanding of the situation. We sent in a specially trained police dog called Zak, who had a camera mounted on its head to recce the building. To ensure that Jack didn't panic or think we were manoeuvring to threaten him, we provided a running commentary of our activity to Jack throughout so that he knew what we were doing and why.

Zak entered the two downstairs rooms methodically and with purpose, just the way he had been trained, turning to the right-hand side and going round the extremities of the room. There was no trace of Jack. The dog team confirmed that the downstairs was secure and that we could progress to the upper floor.

We entered the building and held position at the foot of the stairs. We watched the dog make its way upstairs, ahead of the team. He entered the first room on the left-hand side of the hallway. But the spring-loaded hinges closed behind him, locking him in the bathroom. We could see from the camera mounted on his head that Zak was having a well-deserved drink from somewhere he probably shouldn't have been, which made us all laugh. Just the ticket to break the tension. The team moved upstairs and retrieved Zak safely.

Jack was in the living room at the end of the hallway. I could hear the sound of a television in the background. The team moved forward slowly, behind their ballistic shields, giving Jack calm and constant reassurance. Now we had secured the internal area of the flat we could focus on building rapport, dialogue, empathy, trust and eventually exert some influence on Jack.

As with most successful negotiations, setting the ground rules is just as important as the actual engagement. I told Jack that we would not enter the living room where he was or force a confrontation with him; instead, we would remain where we were until *he* felt it appropriate to come to us. We would not come to him.

Jack immediately tested us to see if we would honour that promise.

In a rage he ran at us, wielding a large sword, and repeatedly smashed it into our protective shields. The team showed remarkable restraint and remained in position, allowing him to exhaust himself through repeated striking. After a while, Jack walked back slowly to the rear wall, sat on the window ledge and said, 'Okay, you stayed at the door, right enough'.

We'd gained the level of trust and respect in that moment which would serve us well in our next dialogue. Jack started to engage, and this gave me the opportunity to figure out what made him tick. As I listened to him, he gave me many clues.

I told him that we were there because we had received reports of a gun being fired out into the street through a window. He lifted his jumper and showed us the gun in the waistband of his trousers. This gesture created a surge of energy amongst the firearms team who shouted, 'WEAPON! WAISTBAND OF TROUSERS!'.

This response is entirely consistent with their training – they need to identify any weapon in order to ensure that every member of the team is immediately aware of any potential threat and where it may come from. However, such a response was de-stabilising to the tranquil atmosphere I was trying to create. I needed to calm the firearms team down and our man – simultaneously.

Calmly, I thanked Jack for showing us the weapon *and* for keeping it in his waistband. I made it clear that any movement towards the weapon would be perceived as a threat. I asked him to help me stabilise the situation, making no sudden movements and keeping our guys calm by behaving calmly himself. He agreed to do this. He told me that as I had kept to my word, he would do likewise as he was 'a man of his word'. I would remember the significance of that phrase and use it as leverage later when it was time to close the deal.

We shifted the discussion onto the impact of the drugs Jack had taken. I needed to signal to our entire team that our client was thinking and speaking lucidly. We were now having a rational conversation and this benefited everyone involved.

To reassure Jack that he was working with a professional, I told him I had safely resolved many siege incidents like this in the past. And that, with his help, we would be able to do the same on this occasion. We just needed to understand and trust each other as we were putting our lives in each other's hands. Although it was becoming an easier conversation, it was important for everyone to acknowledge the risks.

Jack started to tell me his story. He was a player in Glasgow's criminal underworld. A rival figure had been imprisoned and a power vacuum had been created in the local organised crime setup. Firing his weapon sent a message to those who would seek to kill him that he was anything but defenceless and any attack would be met with deadly force.

I noticed that during this dialogue he repeatedly raised his voice so that it was audible to the TV and newspaper reporters who, inevitably, had parked outside just beyond the police cordon. He could actually see himself on his TV and was pleased with the live coverage he was getting. This gave him a platform from which to advise his would-be adversaries that he would fiercely defend both his territory and his crew and would not be frightened by threats on his life. Quite the contrary – it was *them* who should be in fear of their lives as he knew the names of his enemies. He said he would ensure they could no longer pose a threat to him or his people.

Seeing what he was doing, I realised that my initial assessment of the situation was at odds with what was really going on. It's a very valuable lesson to *focus on the other person's perspective, not your own, so that you get an appreciation of the real situation rather than one built on supposition and incomplete information.*

My initial assessment had been that I was dealing with a violent, high, aggressive male who posed a risk to everyone. But now I was looking at a man filled with bravado who was hiding his own fear – he was a very frightened man. To the outside world, his body language and words gave the impression he was fearless and threatening. A more perceptive interpretation was that he was in a corner and looking for a way out of the mess he was in.

On the face of it we wanted very different outcomes. He wanted to get out of there and I wanted him to be arrested. I searched for a common goal to connect us. Our lowest common denominator was that we *both* wanted him to stay alive, and if we could enhance his status with his own crew and amongst his enemies simultaneously, an agreement could be reached. It would involve a prison sentence, probably in the region of ten years, so I needed to inform him of the likely outcome and then sell him on it.

Quietly, I summarised what I had picked up from the conversation:

'When you are confronted directly you will fight. But you don't really want to kill someone or die yourself, do you? This is about your own status, your ability to defend your own crew. That's what this is all about, isn't it? You need your crew to hear and believe that you will protect them and your turf to the death!'

'Exactly!', he replied.

That response told me I had connected with a level of precision that would allow me to close the deal and so I took the opportunity to present a solution which would meet his needs.

'If we can work together to send a clear message to everyone that you are not to be messed with, then that would achieve your goal, yes? Part of that message will be to your crew and family, and part of that will be to your enemies.'

He agreed.

There was just one obstacle. The presence of his weapon would prevent us from entering the room and therefore prevent any resolution. It would also prevent the media from getting close-up videos and pictures when he was arrested. He would, therefore, need to surrender his gun if we were going to make his status-enhancing arrest.

I told Jack what we needed him to do. He walked over to the far corner of the room and told us that he would place his weapon on the ground. The armed officers gave him clear instructions so that at no point would the weapon be pointed at anyone. The surrender of the weapon was the most intense few seconds – the most dangerous moment for our team is always when someone has their hands on or near a loaded weapon. Once Jack placed his weapon on the ground and walked away, he created a space where we could get between him and the weapon to prevent him getting access to it again.

It was over.

I asked Jack to lie down in the far corner of the room and start faking drug-induced sleepiness. The firearms commander was aware of what was going on and that this was going to be a choreographed arrest. What was happening now was a show for the TV cameras. One that allowed us to end the crisis and Jack to keep face with those he needed to impress.

Two members of the firearms squad entered the room and recovered the weapon. Now the location was secure. We ushered the TV crews in front of the house ready to film the live arrest.

We allowed our man to run around the room smashing things up so he looked like he was brave enough to fight six armed officers single-handedly. To add to the drama, Jack shouted, 'Come on – come and fight, you cowards!' He threw his television out of the window and smashed a large vase – whispering to us *sotto voce* that he had always hated the vase and laughing under his breath. He was handcuffed, arms behind his back and, looking bruised and a bit bloodied, was frogmarched outside to the waiting cameras.

All of which goes to show you can't believe everything you see on the television news!

Jack got ten years in prison.

Negotiation lessons

I was 'selling' Jack on the prospect of ten years behind bars. Jack 'bought' this by laying down his firearm and allowing us to make a safe arrest. I painted a compelling vision of his future where he would be the central character in his own story; positioning him as the head of a criminal organisation arrested at gunpoint would ensure that his reputation would be enhanced. He would walk out into the sun after a 24-hour siege to face the waiting media with his dignity intact. Which, in turn, guaranteed his safety from those who may seek to kill him on the outside. We had been willing to facilitate this because we understood *why* he needed such an outcome and because *it was an affordable price to pay* for the peaceful resolution of a potentially lethal situation.

In truth, I didn't sell him ten years in prison. I found out his real motivations and packaged them in a way that gave him a relevant outcome. Listening to him properly, asking him the right questions, noticing his behaviour and demonstrating trustworthiness allowed this to happen. It all makes sense if you understand the context and exercise empathy with the client's situation.

Not all our stories are as extreme as this one. But we wanted to kick off with a story that shows the attitude and behaviour you should always arm yourself with in any negotiation. Your plan won't always play out the way you intend. So, instead of planning everything based on assumptions and stratagems, be *prepared* mentally, emotionally and practically. Then, whatever comes your way, you'll be better able to cope, re-evaluate and apply to get the best possible outcome.

CHAPTER 2

Hidden value or hidden secrets?

'When you have eliminated the impossible, whatever
remains, however improbable, must be the truth'
SHERLOCK HOLMES, *THE SIGN OF FOUR*

In negotiations we are very often confronted by the opening position
adopted by our counterparts. When they use hardball tactics it usually
means that they are more powerful than us or are not mandated to move
from that position.

Most of the time, your counterparts' *anchored position* is their
opening offer. They are hiding their true limitations from you, trying to
get the best deal for themselves. People hide things for a variety of
reasons, but the difference between negotiating and haggling is that in
negotiation we understand their 'secret', undeclared needs and the true
nature of where the best solution lies.

Negotiators' expertise comes from being able to reveal that
hidden element. Haggling usually entails going around and around on
issues, particularly cost, without looking at wider considerations or
making much progress.

On one occasion, I was contacted by someone from the
humanitarian sector who had been in contact with a reputable
journalist working in Iraq. She was covering the story of a local boy from
Baghdad who had been kidnapped by criminals. They were demanding
ransom money from his father.

The young boy had been kidnapped seven months earlier when

walking to school with his sister. She was unharmed during the abduction and left alone. The journalist had come across the story and decided to help by seeking professional negotiators to assist.

The father had been successful in the oil industry but his corrupt business partner had embezzled funds and, after being exposed, had fled the company, leaving our client to deal with the mess. The local mafia knew about the missing money and wanted their cut of the loot. So they kidnapped our client's son to get information about where the money was hidden from his father, our client.

Our client received a series of demands with accompanying videos showing his son in great distress. These came shortly after a hand grenade had been lobbed into his garden. Our client was justifiably terrified – using grenades merely to intimidate, with total disregard for any consequences, showed the extraordinary level of threat to our client and his family.

The mafia claimed to be relocating the boy regularly to avoid detection by the security forces. They mocked the police's efforts and seemed to be one step ahead of them at every turn. Our client was convinced that the whole thing was being choreographed in a corrupt alliance between the mafia and the law enforcement agents – it was common knowledge that bribery and corruption were rife within the government and security services within Iraq. So when our client was allocated an armed guard by the security forces, he was suspicious that, in reality, the security detail was there to spy on him rather than to protect him.

The kidnappers were asking for $800,000. Whilst our client was wealthy in terms of the average Iraqi citizen, he only had $5000 savings. The kidnappers must have known this; so what did they *really* want, we asked ourselves?

Things were being hidden by all sides.

We must always guard against looking at things through our own biased prism, but instead try to visualise and understand the perspective of others.

This was never so apparent as when our client received a call from the kidnappers where they threatened to kill his son. Our client remained calm and said that if that happened then it would be the will of Allah. I could not imagine being so calm and resilient when the life of my son was at stake.

Our client's response really brought home to us that this was a very complex negotiation, replete with subtlety and cultural nuance. Outside of Iraq society, with a completely different philosophical tradition and an entirely alien set of ethical and behavioural values, we were clearly at a disadvantage.

I tried to work out what the hidden needs of each party might be. I had to figure out not just the concealed facts but also why they were being hidden.

Over the years, I have found that the harder people try to conceal information, the more obvious it becomes. The bigger the wall you build around something, the more visible it becomes and the more curious I am to look over it to see what needs protecting so much.

I started looking at where the wall was being built. Within the overall story there were several elements that required clarification.

- Why was the son taken and not the daughter?
- What was my client's relationship with the corrupt business partner?
- Why did the mafia think my client had more money than what showed in his bank balance? What was his true level of wealth?
- Was the government complicit?
- What did my client need to hide from the bodyguard allocated by the security forces?
- Is the use of grenades a normal way to get information?
- Why were the mafia playing cat and mouse?
- Was each area they moved the kidnapped son to as safe as the last one?

Negotiators don't challenge such issues. If we believe deception is taking place, we just push the parties further into their lies and gradually destabilise them to find out why the story is being told this way.

By doing this we got to the truth – eventually.

Our client had embezzled the money. He was trying to keep it and was prepared to risk his son rather than hand it back. His mysterious business partner was in fact his brother-in-law, a man who knew that our client had taken the money. The brother-in-law was the kidnapper. Our client was using us to find out how much the security services knew about him. As he clearly knew, the security services suspected our client's involvement.

The son was released alive, having gone through something no nine-year-old boy should ever have to experience.

We had been negotiating with the kidnappers in good faith but our client had concealed his relationship to them because of his desire to retain his embezzled funds. The journalist was upset that she had been supporting him for months because she had believed his story. Her only fault was looking through her own prism, not believing that another human being could behave so despicably.

Negotiation lessons

Take every opportunity to explore for hidden value.

In the world of negotiation, the search for hidden value and shared goals is at the epicentre of all conflict situations we have resolved.

As a hostage negotiator, I often found myself in situations where people were adamant that their perspective was the correct one – in fact, the only one. In negotiation we recognise that the position adopted by the other side is:

– probably what they would desire in a perfect world
– different from what they would settle for, and
– definitely different from what they actually need.

Hostage-takers make demands for one thing but really need something completely different.

Get over your own preconceptions, assumptions and beliefs. Other people don't see the world the same way as you do. They will often bring a whole set of cultural, ethical and perceptual norms to the situation that are entirely alien to your own. So take nothing for granted, question everything, remain alert to clues and always ask yourself: what's *really* going on here?

PART 1: SUMMARY

Remember that the foundation of every successful negotiation is empathy. Before we move on to part 2, here is a summary of the key lessons we've learned so far. No matter the context, use them in your interactions to set yourself up for success:

Empathy

Empathy is the recognition and articulation of another person's emotional state and their context.

It is not:

- walking in the other person's shoes
- feeling their pain
- sympathising with them
- solving their problems

In order to progress towards mutual agreement and understanding, we need to make our counterpart feel heard and understood – we must empathise with them. Only then will they be open to what we have to say.

Consider the other person's/party's perspective

It is not enough to plan a negotiation based on assumptions and stratagems; we must be prepared mentally, emotionally and practically. This means we must focus on the other person's perspective, not our own, so that we can appreciate the full situation rather than one built on supposition and incomplete information.

Your counterpart's opening offer is usually their 'anchored position'. This is:

- probably what they would desire in a perfect world

- different from what they would settle for, and
- definitely different from what they actually need.

Try to visualise and understand the perspective of others, rather than assessing the situation through the prism of your own biases. If there are cultural and/or ethical differences between you and your counterpart, try to discover what values, morals and behaviours they value.

Try to understand why they desire a specific outcome and what their needs are. Uncover their real motivations and create an outcome or solution that is relevant to this. For some people, reputation is as important as remuneration; it isn't always about money.

The search for shared goals and hidden value is at the centre of all conflict resolution. What could they be hiding that would reveal a solution that is acceptable to both parties? Take nothing for granted, ask questions, remain alert to clues and **always ask yourself: what's *really* going on here?**

Look for inconsistencies in their motivations and the story they tell you. If you notice deception, you should not challenge them but push them to elaborate. This will destabilise them and help reveal why the story is being told this way.

PART 2

We Plan, God Laughs: Being Resourceful Under Pressure

There is a well-known military saying that 'no battle plan survives contact with the enemy'. Many people, especially in business, love to plan. They like to create perfect models for how they will conduct operations. These 'perfect world' scenarios often fail to take into account the reaction of competitors, disruptive influences in the market or sudden changes in circumstance, and, consequently, end up consigned to the waste-paper basket of history.

In negotiation, you cannot really plan, but you can *prepare*. The better you do your homework, the more chances you have to play the game well; the more flexible and adaptable you are, the quicker and more agile you can be.

Shit happens – know that it will. Deal with it, by becoming more resourceful; don't let it crush your spirit just because it doesn't fit with your plan.

Take this situation, for example.

Six mentally ill patients had taken control of the roof of the main building at the local hospital and were refusing to come down.

We had worked hard to understand the dynamics between all six people, ensuring that they did not harm each other. When we finally established credibility with them, I promised them all a hot meal if they, in exchange, would come down off the roof.

When the hot food order arrived at the front door I communicated to them that I had kept my word and that they should do likewise. They said they hadn't received the food. I went to investigate. The firearms team, who were deployed just outside the front door, had assumed the fish and chips were for them and ate the lot.

The siege lasted another eight hours . . .

CHAPTER 3

Dealing with an eleventh-hour curveball

Turin, Italy. Ten o'clock in the evening. After a long day travelling, I was ready for sleep. After all, tomorrow was a big day. We were buying a great company. Sipping the last of my wine after a delicious dinner with my colleague, we heard a ping on our phones – notification of an email. Having just put the finishing touches to the agenda for our morning meeting with two Italian cousins, whose company we were buying, I reluctantly opened my mailbox.

The email was from our boss, the Group CFO, based in New York. In his usual terse communication style, and ignoring the time difference between the Eastern seaboard of the USA, where it was only 4pm, and Italy, where business was well done for the day, he instructed us to downgrade our purchase from 100 per cent to just 60 per cent of the cousins' business – and to complete the deal in the morning as planned.

We'd worked with the CFO long enough to be certain that a call with him would be a waste of time. A giant hole had just opened up in front of us. My energy was low and the clock was now ticking.

I was all for sitting the cousins down over a beer and telling them that, reluctantly, we were out. That there wasn't going to be any deal. My colleague was having none of that defeatist talk, however. He refused to give up without at least making a proposal. He wasn't the type to be fazed by an eleventh-hour curveball. Compared to the wild stories he'd shared with me about his time running Eastern European nightclubs in the early nineties, this was *una passeggiata nel parco* – a stroll in the park.

Changing the terms of the deal at the last minute might have felt easy to my colleague but it felt like a mountain to climb for me. I'd been the one entrusted with building a close working relationship with the two cousins for the nine months leading up to this point. The deal had become a pact of trust between us all – not just between the two cousins and me, but also with members of their family (this was Italy, after all). Not to mention the large groups of company employees and family friends. I'd also been right down in the detail of the financial negotiation and all the legalities for several months too. The t's had been crossed and the i's dotted on this deal and it was carefully constructed on a foundation of hard-earned trust. I had personally poured a great deal of effort into building the relationship, which ran way beyond the legal niceties, and my own integrity with the Italians was on the line. Such a huge U-turn at the last minute felt like a fatal blow. We were already emotionally and physically spent, and with this degree of deal fatigue and emotional investment the situation felt hopeless.

It was a long night. We used a lot of flip-chart paper to work out how to make our case sound attractive enough to the cousins that they would go ahead.

By the next morning we had neat versions of the flip charts ready to go. We glued on our best espresso-fuelled smiles and greeted the sellers and their advisor enthusiastically as they walked into the room. The only way to successfully present this was as a good news story. To keep looking them in the eye, tell and show them how much better this deal would be for everyone.

We began.

We were met with stony faces. We kept going with our sales pitch and flip charts. When we finished there was a pause and then the predictable and entirely understandable '*WTF!?*' reaction. We'd anticipated this. This was the decisive moment. And we knew what to do. *Keep quiet, listen attentively and show that we understood where they were coming from. We had to absorb their anger in order to let the heat out of the room so everyone could refocus.*

These guys were a class act. Born negotiators. They knew the game. They wanted to find a way to make this happen, so it would cost us. But there would be a way.

We went back to basics. I walked their advisor through the numbers again. After years working with him, the cousins had total faith in this man, so they left us to it. We went through his long list of questions. He needed to give his clients a view, mainly about whether what we had done was anything other than the most cynical kind of 'bait and switch' scam – a classic con trick to excite interest and get to a deal, only to reduce the offer at the last minute in order to get a better price when it's too late to back out.

We were buying using an 'earnout' – where the total price we would ultimately pay depends on the delivery of agreed levels of profit in the future produced by the company we are buying. The cousins' company was projecting high levels of continued growth and profitability, so they'd created an environment where, if their projections were correct, holding on to 40 per cent of the company would, ultimately, make them even more money than if we bought the full 100 per cent now. And, as they were also men of honour, they would deliver their own financial projections – wouldn't they?

We broke for the traditional Torinese lunch. This gave several hours for the cousins and their advisor to discuss the different scenarios before meeting up with us again in the early evening.

As youngsters the cousins had had it tough. Brought up by single parents, they were raised on a run-down estate and made their pocket money by distributing free-sheet newspapers to metro commuters. One of them had suffered a truly traumatic relationship breakdown where his wife had deserted him for his best friend not too long into the marriage.

They relied on trust but, unsurprisingly, had massive trust issues. So they needed proof when dealing with relatively unknown potential partners. They needed independent validation and they needed to look you deep in the eye. We passed all those tests and we got the deal done – but not the next day. It took several more weeks. We did buy 60 per cent of their company – but redefined what the deal meant for them in the long run.

The extra time was needed to:

- regain trust
- give them time to look at the deal through a totally different lens, and
- negotiate with our boss, the group company CFO, to define what '60 per cent' actually meant. That way, we could deliver something to the cousins that was still really 100 per cent by guaranteeing terms on the remaining 40 per cent at a later date.

Negotiation lessons

The trust and relationship you build with each other during a negotiation are the bedrock of doing a deal. They are usually necessary prerequisites of making a deal happen. But they are especially important when you're within inches of the finishing line and an eleventh-hour curveball is thrown your way.

When things don't go to plan, sometimes you need extra time. Take the time. Invest that additional time in the relationship and in re-building trust. And use the extra time to be creative – re-formulate and re-configure the deal. Creativity takes time.

CHAPTER 4

It's not my hand grenade, it's yours

I got off the plane in an all-too-familiar JFK on a Sunday evening two weeks before Independence Day. Having spent so much time away from my family working on the deal, I consoled myself with the fact that I'd be home just as the schools break up for the summer holidays, able to relax and celebrate.

Like 99 per cent of the people in the immigration line, as soon as I could get a signal on my phone I was on my email. The meeting with the lawyers was due to start early the next morning so I planned to put my enforced one-hour slot in the queue to good use by clearing my inbox.

Before I could get to my emails, I saw an alert that I had a new voicemail. This was unusual as almost every message in the world now seems to be written – it feels as though, in this age of AI, we humans are increasingly losing the ability to talk to each other. The message started cheerfully enough, but soon turned sour. It stated that the $100m of cash we were due to get paid when the deal was closed at the end of the week had been reduced to just $50m. The message continued, stating that the buyer would make up the difference by issuing us a 'loan note' – which is basically an I.O.U. It finished with some story about the banks being unwilling to provide the debt to fund all the cash.

What was going on? What was really behind this? I had only the taxi ride to my hotel to formulate a plan. My clients were due to be waiting for me in the lobby.

My two principal clients were maverick and could be

confrontational but they were also very savvy. They'd both mentally spent the $100m they were due to be paid (and the further $25m that was due to follow if they hit their targets).

With the taxi drawing up to the hotel it was time to focus. Was this still the best deal? Still a good deal? Yes. It may always have been the buyer's intention to halve the cash element. But thinking like that would get us nowhere. Trashing the buyer in front of my client and railing against them for this underhand move was more likely to blow up the deal than get it done on terms we could accept. Conversely, positioning this as good news, or even neutral, would have lacked credibility.

I decided to opt for blaming the banks. After all, banking markets can do shitty things with no forewarning, leaving our buyer in a difficult position, so the debt problem was credible. Blaming the banks might sound like a cop-out, but placing blame on them was the right route to go, I reasoned. In fact, it was probably the only route.

If you're negotiating alone, it's easy to talk yourself into dark corners. My paranoid mind went into overdrive. My clients were already very wealthy guys. They liked money. And they were very keen to get much more of it. Surely they would be furious about this and take it out on me? I had to find a way to stop them from crucifying me.

I walked up to them at the hotel bar and told them straight how it was: the voicemail, what it meant and how we should deal with it. As a pair of wheeler-dealers, they had been surprised we'd got this far without an event like this. And they had been deeply suspicious it hadn't. (They'd chosen not to tell me in case I somehow signalled this to the buyer.)

Now, my clients felt, we were all in the same game. It was a game they recognised and enjoyed playing. The money on the table was still great, so there was no need to be despondent. Nor did we want to blow that. After a few rounds of cocktails the conversation turned to how we could extract the absolute maximum possible in all other areas to compensate for this huge reduction in the cash price. We could play this situation to our advantage. The buyer had changed the terms at the last minute but was still keen to do the deal. Having changed the terms so late in the day gave us licence to bring back to the negotiation table a whole bunch of demands we'd traded in order to reach the original deal.

That evening allowed us to reset and focus. Battle lines were drawn and at breakfast we redrew them more calmly, putting this current situation in the context of the whole deal. After all, this was only the start of the investment period – we'd have several years to extract full payback. (We didn't have to have it all at the initial close.) Years we fully intended to use to our advantage.

Negotiation lessons

The CIA has an unofficial motto: *'Know what you need to know before you believe what you want to believe.'* It's a good reminder not to convince ourselves that our own perspective is correct or accurate – to be guilty of 'wishful thinking'.

On the other hand, it is easy to convince ourselves that everything is a disaster, that we will be hung out to dry. Especially when we are on our own in a negotiation and can only rely on our own inner monologue.

When the negotiation's moving along nicely, keep asking yourself, 'What is the worst thing that could blow up in my face?' and 'What am I not seeing here?'. And have options to tackle those scenarios.

Equally, when things don't go to plan, put on your metaphorical optimistic hat and think of all the *advantages* this new situation provides you with.

CHAPTER 5

Lipstick on a pig (beware groupthink)

One of my abiding childhood memories is of having to miss school with flu in January 1986. This meant time on the sofa watching one of the four TV channels available in the UK at that time. I lucked out – they were showing a Space Shuttle launch and I was glued to the screen. Like so many people's experience that fateful day, my excitement turned to horror as I watched the *Challenger* explode on live TV. Investigations ultimately showed the devastating role that defective decision-making processes – *groupthink* – played in that tragedy.

Groupthink often has a toxic role in negotiations. What feels like an aggressive, calculated stance from the opposing negotiating team may not be intentional at all. It can sometimes simply be the result of a group of people talking themselves into a position from which they can't even see they need an escape. Calling out such behaviour is hard and can feel very risky. But you must be that person. Call it out.

A common feature of corporate mergers and acquisitions is 'preparing for exit' – the time *preceding* the actual sale process. It involves lots of important groundwork, which can take months, to ensure a smooth sales process and to get all the stakeholders properly aligned around the potential transaction and what it will involve.

It is also a period, however, where the principals in the deal can let their expectations for the value of the transaction – and the speed at which it will happen – spiral totally out of control. To make matters worse, in order to support the principals' inflated expectations of the outcome, advisors try to keep their clients happy by aggressively over-selling the company. This can be effective with uninformed financial investors but strategic buyers will see right through it and run a mile.

Our firm of advisors is known as a team of deep industry experts. We're quite often asked to come in and give an off-the-record view. A few years ago, we were called in by a prospective investor. They were interested in a company operating in a sector with which they were quite familiar – but they couldn't make sense of what they were seeing. Their assessment was based on a standard suite of sale materials that bankers prepare: a presentation on the company, a market study prepared by independent consultants and a gigantic pack of financial models. On the surface this analysis should show a class-leading business growing much faster than its market. But it didn't.

To people in the know and not afraid to give a direct point of view, the firm in question was being misrepresented by its advisors. The mooted value was not at all justified. The potential buyer had read the many hundreds of pages of market and commercial diligence written by top-name advisors but their lingering gut concerns were unchanged – and spot-on.

Starting a negotiation on price rarely works when a seller has, for months, been told they're worth way more than the market will deliver. Whilst this was not the investment opportunity that had been represented, it still had excellent potential – if done on a totally different basis and with a totally different post-deal strategy. This would necessarily mean a different price and different terms. There was no point sugar-coating it and it was our duty to make our assessment crystal clear. But this message had to be delivered with empathy; and, due to the chasm in expectations that had been forming for so long, with an accompanying 'Plan B' to demonstrate a way to achieve the desired outcome.

I've seen many friends caught out in the housing market by agents reassuring them that the price they list their property at should be set at a level that beggars belief. This is followed by almost no buyer interest or a weak trickle of insulting low-ball offers. Over the course of months, with real market feedback, and some frank chats with mates over a pint at the pub putting the world to rights, they recapture their initial reaction to the listing price and realise that they fell for it. Maybe at that point they can re-list, but sometimes the damage is permanent and renting rather than selling is the only way out.

The driving force in this instance was the ownership structure of the target company. It was majority-owned by an investor who had run out of patience with a management team who weren't achieving growth at the target rate (contrary to what we were being told). The management team remained passionate about making progress with a company they'd built over many years and who knew that a new investor would be their best shot. What everyone needed was a believable business plan that management could sell to themselves, their current and prospective investors. And a new voice at the table – us – keeping a sense of perspective for everyone concerned. To shine a light on how everyone had inadvertently ended up in this mess and to validate a way out with fair terms for all parties.

Initially, the seller dug in his heels and refused to give up on any of his key financial demands or deadlines. But as deadlines came and went with no consequences, other than some aggressive posturing on phone calls, we could run our own process to our own timetable. The seller's behaviour and failure to recognise that the game was up probably cost him rather than improved his return.

Together, we worked up a compelling plan that galvanised the management team and the buyer in terms of their vision for the business and its future opportunity. The exercise of co-developing the plan brought them together as a unit. This left the seller isolated. He had to accept that the management team had mentally moved on and the deal, on the terms that we proposed, now needed to proceed.

Negotiation lessons

When you know that the game is up, continuing to dig your heels in is going to cost you more than it will gain you. Instead, recognise and accept that circumstances have changed and move into closing mode. We've all seen the special forces reality shows where they simulate interrogation techniques. Every time, without fail, even the toughest reach breaking point. The best – and those that get their team out alive – are the ones who pick their moment to 'break'.

Most negotiations aren't carried out one on one. One of the greatest barriers you will need to break is the groupthink factor. Don't be afraid to stand up if you are the only dissenting voice in a collective who are absolute in their conviction. The power of 'What if' questions is immense in this scenario. 'What if we weren't looking at this right?' You're not breaking ranks but asking the group to pause and reflect, and at least giving the group a ladder with which to climb down from your position, should you need to.

CHAPTER 6

Help your rival get past issues that affect you both

There are so many schools of deal-making and negotiation. Psychology, gameplay, warfare even. Generally, however, they involve some sense of 'them and us' – a winner and a loser. Of course, there's the totally contradictory school of thought that deals and negotiation are most successful when they're collaborations rather than confrontations. We prefer the latter.

I once had a boss who, to me, perfectly summed up how best to think about the negotiating dynamic. He told me that we should always be in love with the companies we bought, but that we could only allow ourselves to fall in love from the moment we signed the deal. Until that point we're not on the same side and we must always keep asking ourselves 'why?'.

We were in a negotiation to buy a fantastic company that filled a major gap in our capabilities, had a great leadership team and made very good profits. They presented themselves to us perfectly; they ticked every box we could wish for. We saw this as a deal to close as quickly as possible. The sellers were so confident that this was the right deal for them they were speaking to us exclusively – pretty much unheard of in our world.

We agreed the headline terms of the deal quickly and moved straight into due diligence and drafting the legal contracts. Which was when life got a whole lot more interesting, very quickly.

Most services businesses require little cash funding to launch and scale. Unlike manufacturing or technology businesses, they're not capital intensive. If they're fortunate enough to win a major client early on, that client income can be their main way to fund growth. Even so, a little funding to get the company off the ground can take some of the pressure off the founders. A few thousand dollars can feel like a useful safety net while the business establishes itself. This kind of funding seldom comes from banks or other financial institutions because their capital is at risk. It tends to be from a friend, former colleague or family member – which can make it horribly awkward to negotiate terms or suggest that a lawyer needs to draft something 'proper' for everyone (just in case it's needed in the future).

I would argue that if we were the traditional 'enemy' – by virtue of sitting on the opposite side of the negotiating table – we were playing it with a completely straight bat. This was patently clear to the sellers in every interaction and they repeatedly told us as much. We were a *collaborative* enemy and the deal was moving efficiently without any hitches.

We'd convened for the traditional 'all parties' negotiation meeting with the lawyers and other advisors to discuss our due diligence findings and the key points on the legal contracts. Unusually, the two main sellers were late, and when they arrived there was only one of them.

'What's up?' we asked.

'One of our original investors has just reneged on a handshake deal we did years ago about what he would personally make from any exit. He says he wants a full share of the proceeds.'

We were straight shooters and had been throughout. They knew that the price we'd agreed was fixed so the extra money the silent shareholder was now demanding would have to come from the sellers' share of the proceeds. But when they'd said yes to our deal it wasn't based on the total value of the deal. Instead, it was calculated on how much each of them would *personally* receive. They had no wiggle room.

This investor's demand would make a big hole in the money the other sellers would make – to the extent that it would negate the point of the deal. We weren't the enemy but we couldn't just crank up the price to fill the hole.

Our meeting room was on the sixth floor and out of the window we could see the main shareholder sitting on the pavement down below with his feet in the road and his head in his hands. Broken. A deal he'd been working towards for a decade was snatched from him at the eleventh hour by someone who'd been his friend and helped get the business underway. My boss spotted our broken man on the pavement and went straight down to him. He put his arm around the guy's shoulder and told him very calmly that we'd make this problem go away. He told him to take a few minutes, compose himself and, when he was ready, join us in the room as there was a great deal to be done.

The problem was sizeable: a £1 million hole in the proceeds that needed fixing. We could be of help in that process.

We knew the silent investor in question and knew that, while money was important to him, reputation was a very close second. We went into charm offensive mode. Serious flattery from our best-known senior executives – high-profile 'names' in adland – over a couple of lunches, balanced with a respectful warning about the reputational damage dishonourable behaviour could cause in such a close-knit industry, quickly opened up a conversation about a route forward. People who claim to be 'honourable' generally care about their reputation and attach a value to it. This value can be disproportionate to financial value.

It didn't take more than a few days – nor did it cost anything close to the £1 million – to unblock the situation. We may not have been the author of the problem, but by being an ally to our new partners – by helping them find a resolution – we had considerable moral credit in the bank. Which got our relationship off to a terrifically strong start.

Negotiation lessons

Focus on the issues that affect you both. Find the common ground, even if you are on 'different sides' in the negotiation. Acting honourably and helping the other side get past problems that impact you both smooths the path to a deal and sets you up well for future partnership.

PART 2: SUMMARY

You can't plan for everything that might happen in a negotiation – there are simply too many variables – but you can ensure that you are mentally prepared for sudden changes. Remember these key lessons and the old adage 'shit happens':

Mental preparation

The more flexible and adaptable you are, the quicker and more agile you can be when something you weren't expecting happens.

Throughout the negotiation, continually ask yourself, 'What is the worst thing that could happen?' and 'What am I not seeing here?'. Come up with answers to those questions so that you are prepared for curveballs.

If you're negotiating alone, it's easy to talk yourself into dark corners. Seek counsel from people whose opinion you trust. Different perspectives will reveal new options to try and help you see a more balanced view of the situation.

Interacting with the other party amid chaos

If you are going to weather the storm of unexpected events, establishing trust is essential. Showing empathy and recognising the other party's needs helps form a bedrock of trust.

When you are dealt a bad hand – for example, a U-turn at the eleventh hour – keep a level head and look for the positives. Go back to the basics: regain trust, allow yourself or your counterpart the time to look at the deal through a new lens.

In chaotic circumstances, emotions can run high. Rash decisions in these moments can blow up the deal altogether. Keep quiet, listen attentively and show empathy. Sometimes you have to absorb the other party's anger in order to let the heat out of the room so everyone can refocus.

Focus on the issues that affect you both. Find the common

ground, even if you are on different sides in the negotiation. Acting honourably and helping the other side get past problems that impact you both smooths the path to a deal and sets you up well for future partnership.

Look for silver linings. If your counterpart has moved the goalposts at the last minute, you may be able to redraw the lines in other areas and extract the maximum possible value.

PART 3

Power Imbalances, Dodgy Dealers and Difficult Negotiations

'A smile will get you far, but a smile and a gun will get you further'
– AL CAPONE

You are never solely in charge. There is always at least one more party in a negotiation. Sometimes they, rightly or wrongly, believe they hold the power and behave accordingly. This can range from friendly opposition to haggling, arm-wrestling and even aggressive confrontation.

Don't get dragged into that territory. Get out of the boxing ring and bring yourself and your counterpart to the negotiation table.

Elements of manipulation enter negotiations all the time. In fact some of them sneak into conversations we have every day: praise, scolding, pleading, half-truths, intellectual bullying, using complicated words or jargon, empty promises and bossy demands. You get the picture. You have probably noticed some manipulative moments in many of our previous stories. Here we want to demonstrate how damaging consistent manipulation can be for those who use it and also explain why and how you should stop it before you can continue negotiations.

Whenever we come up against a negotiation partner who is employing hardball tactics, it's usually because they feel that they have nothing to lose. They are emboldened by their one-sided assessment of the situation, which makes them feel powerful. It also makes them less likely to think and behave in a reasonable manner. Arrogance and self-awareness seldom go hand in hand.

Our job is to change that mindset.

In armed siege resolution, we often find that negotiation skills receive a welcome boost when we are backed up by an armed response team. We have faced many reckless and dangerous people who display the courage of a lion, only for that to change a short time later when faced with their own demise.

But what do you do when you don't have an armed response unit by your side?

We must be patient and think strategically. The hardball stance is usually a front that we can reveal with time and then overcome by leveraging the other party's vulnerability, which they usually think is hidden.

CHAPTER 7

Dealing with people who think they hold all the cards

Ego is not a bad thing. It is an essential element of drive and success, an important factor in life and in the world of business. But when ego is overly inflated it can be a problem, particularly when it gets into macho shows of strength. Those who have 'nuclear weapons' often think they hold all the cards – there are live examples of this in international relations right now. But that's not negotiating, it's manipulation. The only way to deal with an over-inflated ego is to ignore the deck of cards they are offering so you can conduct real negotiations instead, based on a different set of cards.

When 'bad actors' are in the game – those people with bad intentions who just want to harm their opponents or squeeze their partners to the point of extinction – you need a strategy to deal with it. Our philosophy is based around the controlled use of power, because merely being nice is not enough for someone whose natural instinct is to take advantage.

> *It is justified to use power and leverage obtained during the negotiation process to adversely affect the success of bad actors in the game.*

There's a Glaswegian phrase: *'don't mistake saftness for daftness',* which means 'don't mistake kindness for stupidity'. What it implies is that you must always possess an iron fist inside a velvet glove.

But there will always be people who seek to take advantage of kindness. Therefore, *we must always be armed with options to use force or leverage as a last resort.*

When I was working with the police, when we were faced with those who physically threaten others, our show of force would always be greater. If the other side didn't think that we would ever use the force that we had at our disposal, it allowed them to visualise a way out of the situation with the best possible outcome for them.

When we made it clear that they had a choice between acting in a reasonable manner or in a way that would necessitate us to respond with force, any subsequent loss would be self-inflicted.

Every time I attended a siege, I presented myself as a reasonable person who was willing to give people space to express themselves. When they felt heard and understood they would start to behave in a reasonable manner and we were able to find a solution. But, make no mistake, I always entered those discussions with the armed siege team behind me, who were ready to exert a different kind of influence should that be required.

When I advised US law enforcement on conflict resolution, my approach was also informed by that philosophy. When we feel safe and secure, we can exercise restraint, the essential ingredient when facing people in crises. You have to give people time to reach that reasonable space where we can find a solution for both parties.

It is with that mindset that we must approach corporate and day-to-day negotiations. We must always signal that we will work hard to find an amicable solution; but we will also use our expertise to show that we will exploit any vulnerabilities to force the other party to behave in a reasonable manner if necessary. It is amazing how many people choose a peaceful path when the alternative means that they will experience major discomfort!

In a merger and acquisitions environment, the vulnerability is the threat of rival bidders. We will often keep more than one party in the negotiation right up until the last possible moment, so that if the preferred party starts playing games we can credibly threaten to drop them for another bidder.

We must aim to cultivate a reputation for fairness. Fairness means that good intentions are rewarded and the relationships we build can flourish. Conversely, bad intentions on the part of others should be punished. Kindness and understanding are our first choice – but not our only one – and a show of restraint is much more powerful when it is seen as one of many options available to us.

CHAPTER 8

Shifting the perceived power imbalance

Moving the perceived power imbalance in your favour is often described as the most difficult challenge in negotiations to overcome. I am often contracted by organisations to negotiate on their behalf when they feel that the odds are stacked against them and they cannot afford to lose.

In all my time as a hostage negotiator, the balance of power was never in my favour – at the beginning.

Every guy with a gun and every person on the ledge of a bridge had the power. Yet by the end of our encounters, I had removed the threats that their power enabled and thereby removed their power. The change in momentum changed outcomes and I used this to bring situations to a negotiated resolution.

What it took to shift the balance of power was a particular mindset and set of skills.

In one of my first corporate assignments, I was employed to negotiate against a large US-based organisation on a billion-dollar contract dispute. In my initial briefing I was advised that the contract fight had just been lost in the Court of Arbitration in Geneva, who decreed that the contract was watertight and that the outstanding amount should be paid in full by my client, albeit in a series of milestone payments.

I established a team and included both a legal and operational manager to help me face the other side. The other side consisted of three industry experts and four lawyers – three of whom were, according to their website, highly connected and the best in class. I felt slightly out of my depth – the fees these guys commanded were eye-watering – as if I was competing in karaoke against rockstars.

As negotiations commenced all seven of my opponents provided clear opinions on how to resolve the payment dispute backed up by a sound rationale. They clearly had years of experience where the strongest argument defeated the weaker argument and that was their recipe for success.

Naturally, if I had entered that playground, I would have suffered at the hands of such razor-sharp minds and sound legal rationale. Instead, I decided that my best chance was to bring them into *my* playground, where I could gain some tactical advantage.

Of course, when I sought their perspective, I was looking for their Achilles heel – something they probably felt was non-existent given their overwhelming victory in the Court of Arbitration, which they were already displaying on their website.

This supreme self-confidence would be my ally, as they felt no threat from a Glaswegian ex-copper. And because they perceived no threat, they lowered their guard.

They perceived that my only tactic was to seek a delayed payment plan. In fact, I was looking for opportunities to remove their power. With each conversation, they revealed a lot more about their story and that of their client, and when they overexaggerated some aspects, they highlighted the very place I should look for vulnerability.

I found lots of opportunities to explore for leverage, but like a good negotiator, I stored each aspect for later use without revealing my true level of interest. I knew that if I had confronted each item one by one, they would have picked me off and protected their client. When I chose to tip the balance, it needed to feel like a tidal wave.

I was playing a game of patience within a game of poker. I found inconsistencies in their individual stories, and again rather than confront them I stored these to destabilise their position later on.

After months of dialogue, one lawyer asked me for my proposal. He was quite mocking. Laughing, he said, 'None of us understand why you're going on with this! Why are you even here? What is it that you hope to gain from stringing this out? You've already lost in court. What is it that you propose?'

I had validated all that I was about to launch. Their arrogance had revealed a lack of due diligence on their client. A diligence that I had been doing for months and which they validated without knowing. Their client's product was coming out in a highly regulated market and they had claimed that the product already had approval from the regulator. It didn't. Whilst the regulator most likely would give approval, technically, the product not only did not yet have approval, as they had claimed, but the company had also failed to disclose that the product had recently failed the relevant test when they demonstrated it on nationwide television.

I reframed the situation to make the facts they had ignored into a compellingly disastrous case for their client. Leveraging my law enforcement credentials, I pointed out that if these facts were brought to the attention of the FBI – with whom I, as a high-ranking law enforcement officer, had strong connections – a case of high-level corporate fraud with intention to deceive the public would ensue. Which, in turn, could cause the company's major backer, who donated over $200m a year to this firm – to withdraw funding.

I presented what my client had to lose alongside a catastrophically high risk of loss to them – much greater than the billions at stake in the negotiation, which they may be able to recover elsewhere. In other words, I presented them with a disastrous scenario and linked it to a putative escape plan, which they were glad to take. We agreed to 'divorce'; the partnership had run its course and they would allow us to leave without any further payment.

Negotiation lessons

The truth is, I only had a small amount of circumstantial evidence but presented it as fact – their reaction showed me that I had hit the jackpot. This is when I realised that, as in the world of hostage negotiation, so in the corporate world – perception is more powerful than reality.

When it may appear that the other side holds all the cards, shifting perception and using both reason and emotion can often turn a one-sided, highly manipulative situation 180 degrees.

A risk presented as a threat is only valid if it is perceived by your opponent as a thing that can cause actual harm. And timing is as important as impact: when they are thrown off balance is the time to push as you have the momentum.

CHAPTER 9

My dad's bigger than your dad. Negotiating against people who act in bad faith

When I entered the corporate world, it took me some time to identify where I would fit in, but I knew that the skills of hostage negotiation were readily transferable. I had spent a career fighting injustice and dealing with 'bad faith' actors who preyed on the vulnerabilities of others. As the commercial marketplace had become more and more competitive, margins were being squeezed and many companies were under pressure – I could now see similar tactics being used within the corporate world. Less deadly than in hostage situations but identical in intent.

It is only logical that many companies seek to gain advantage. Companies are made up of and represented by human beings, and I have found that human beings are capable of doing incredible things in order to gain power.

I was hired by a client to represent them in a contract negotiation where they were perplexed about the length of time being taken to reach agreement. Dealing with the counterparty company, I was initially unaware that they were acting in bad faith. I had limited experience in this particular industry, which involved complicated technical inventions and patented technology. I did notice that they seemed to be in no particular hurry during our interaction; they claimed that they just wanted to get it right.

Because of my lack of experience in this industry, I relied heavily on my team. They felt that the most likely reason for the other company dragging their feet was that they were waiting for my client's patents to expire. They were running down the time as a delay tactic, hoping that my client would run out of money, resilience or legal protection.

Whilst I was angered by this approach, I knew that showing my emotions and expressing a moral judgement would only disadvantage my client. Realising that our opponents had the funds to fight us in court for a decade, I kept a pleasant disposition.

Each meeting allowed me to profile the other party's words and behaviour and gave me enough evidence to prove to my client that they were acting in bad faith. They intended to put my client out of business to get what they wanted. My client's assessment had been tainted by what she *wanted* to believe the other company was like: honourable. There may well have been honourable people in the organisation but the company's tactics and behaviour were clearly pernicious and harmed those who were less powerful.

Once I had the agreement of my client and she accepted the risks, I put a plan in place to counter the extortion tactics. I realised that my ability to influence them would be limited without leverage. As always, the way to find the vulnerability of an opponent is to shut up and listen. *Sooner or later it will become obvious as they use disproportionate energy to protect it.*

I played the opposition's 'stringing it out' game for another few months. But in the background we threw in our lot with a different company – a much bigger one. An organisation who were already in litigation with our rival and were pursuing hundreds of millions in injunctions against them – and had the financial muscle to do so. We prepared to sell our product to this 'white knight'. They could add our products to their larger legal fight and so strengthen their overall case.

I had stored this leverage for a long time and took great pleasure when I was able to reveal it, neutralising their perception that they had control over us. My opponent arrogantly told me that he had reservations about giving us money now because this would only be used to finance a 'fighting fund' against his patent department. I afforded myself a little smile when I responded by telling him that cash was not our objective and we had secured funds by selling our patents to a richer third party. Our cause had transcended money by now – we would fight for justice by putting a bigger shark in the water next to them!

My arrogant opponent's survival instinct kicked in. The likelihood was that his company would hold him responsible for a failure in the courts which would cost them millions in damages and trash their reputation in the industry. In which case he could end up as a scapegoat and the might he wielded on his employer's behalf would then be turned against him. We settled.

Negotiation lessons

My organisational philosophy revolves around justice, fairness, being reasonable and building partnerships with the other party. But, sometimes, when the other party tries to extort, bully or act in bad faith we need a backup plan in order to help the other party to be reasonable, fair and just. By shifting the ground of the debate and taking the initiative, we can restore balance and negotiate, rather than haggle, manipulate and arm wrestle on their terms. Our team had out-manoeuvred our opponent. We had put together a tight-knit coalition which acted together, and 'I' had become 'we'.

CHAPTER 10

Spotting and stopping manipulation

I was asked to help a woman who had recently become divorced from her partner. They lived in a Middle Eastern country.

As a result of the husband's controlling behaviour, the woman left him and returned to Europe where she began a new life for herself and her daughter. Very often in these situations, the children are caught in the middle and are used as pawns to hurt the other partner.

At first, the relationship was fuelled by conflict. But eventually the husband calmed down, became more reasonable and plausible and asked to visit his child in Spain. He stayed for a few weeks, took the girl out for day trips and won some of the trust necessary to gain unsupervised contact.

One day the father said that he wanted to take his daughter to Disneyland. The mother acquiesced. But instead of travelling to Disneyland, the father had managed to obtain a new passport for his daughter and returned with her to their home in the Middle East.

Once back on home soil the law gave the father an overwhelming advantage in the balance of power.

Now the father held all the cards. He would not allow the mother to see her child physically and started to reduce the number of calls, all of which were supervised. As an absent mother in great distress she often got upset and cried in front of her daughter. Her ex-partner exploited this vulnerability by claiming the mother was upsetting their child thus justifying fewer calls until she had learnt to control her own emotions.

I opened negotiations with the man and confirmed that his only goal should be whatever was in the best interest of his child. My assessment of the father was that he exhibited the personality traits of a narcissistic sociopath. My job was to ensure that the mother did not fall into the traps he laid.

We made him feel in control of the situation, and started to use logical arguments which fitted his narrative to increase access one day at a time.

The argument he had presented meant that, logically, he could not prevent the mother's access if she remained calm and managed her own emotions. His logic became a trap for him as long as we could ensure the mother did this.

Thinking about how to manipulate a manipulator takes a lot of thought, but finding a common objective between the parties is vital. A common objective is the lowest common denominator which shares the interest of both parties, something which yields *mutual* benefit. In this case, the welfare and happiness of the daughter. So if the mother could keep her emotions in check, the agreement to allow calls to the daughter was binding. Especially for a man of honour – which his faith proclaimed him to be.

I sought the assistance of a clinical psychologist whose expertise lay in managing extreme stress and counteracting difficult personality traits and disorders. Over the weeks that followed, the mother got more and more calls with her daughter. It wasn't all that she desired, but it was good enough for now.

In another situation, I was advising an organisation who were in dispute against their industry's trade union. The union was threatening to strike, which would cause financial and reputational harm to the organisation. The union said they would call a vote and the likely outcome of that vote would be in their favour.

Whilst unions are most honourable and they fight valiantly on behalf of often low-paid workers, *sometimes* their officials have a personal agenda. In this case, to instigate strike action and dominate not just the union members but the entire workforce.

The union officials were lobbying the staff to convince their members to strike. They knew that using intimidation tactics and preventing transient workers from voting was not permitted. But that didn't stop it from happening, and many non-unionised workers were afraid to speak out about what was happening.

Intimidation tactics, the classic behaviour of a narcissist.

We got the union to commit, in writing, that they should 'represent the will of the workers' in the full knowledge that they had been, contrarily, suppressing that will in order to achieve their own objective, which was to call a strike. They were now publicly committed to behaving honourably – the very thing that leads to the downfall of negotiators who act in bad faith.

Representing the management, we explained to all of the staff (not just union members) that we were offering a deal which was in the best interests of *everyone*. If the company's budget was breached in a pay settlement that was unaffordable, many hundreds of jobs would be jeopardised. Additionally, if there was a strike, any deal that was reached would take a long time to be agreed and the workers would see nothing of the new pay settlement for months. None of which could ever, surely, be the 'will of the workers'?

To reinforce our direct appeal to the entire workforce, we reminded the union that we would report them to the Central Arbitration Committee (CAC) governing body for manipulation and interference in a voting process if we uncovered any evidence of wrongdoing.

The union never openly conceded defeat. We did not need that outcome; it's important that our partners retain their dignity and save face. But they quietly went about their business, conducted the ballot and ensured that the true will of the workers was reflected in the results. The pay offer went through. We had boxed them into an emotional corner where they could not afford to be seen as acting dishonourably or against the evident interests of the entire workforce – whom they had committed to put above all other considerations.

Negotiation lessons

Before you can even commence a negotiation you must spot if manipulation is happening and take measures to stop it. (Manipulation and negotiation are not the same thing. One mitigates against the other.) Here is what to watch for:

- Creating inequality in positions between you and the other party by using begging, praise, flattery, threat, blackmail or bossing the other party around. In essence, to take up a position where the relationship is one of parent and child rather than adult to adult.
- Appealing to 'moral views' – yours or those of society. For example, appealing to your sense of justice, of right and wrong, asking for honesty or inducing feelings of guilt.
- Lying or twisting the truth, for example saying they feel indignant, offended, cheated, angry, etc.
- Intellectual bullying – too many facts and statistics, too much professional jargon.
- Using bureaucracy as an excuse to tire or annoy.
- Creating stress with unpleasant surprises or physically uncomfortable spaces.
- Commenting on your weaknesses.
- Showing their negative emotions and provoking a conflict.
- Allowing no time to decide.
- Physically or emotionally breaking into your communication comfort zone.

Behaviours like these, where only one side gets all the advantages, are not in your interest and must be stopped because they are always based on exploiting your **weaknesses** and wanting to **control** you.

Here's how to stop manipulation:

Attitude:

1. Know your fundamental rights, which are to have and express your own feelings, opinions and thoughts; to say no; to protect yourself and your interests.

2. Know and define your boundaries. You are fully responsible for yourself but not for others and their happiness, health and wellbeing. Keep your distance.

Techniques:

3. Ask clarifying and probing questions, for example:
– 'Are you asking me or telling me?'
– 'What *exactly* are you unhappy about?'
– 'What *specifically* could we have done differently?'
– 'Do *you* think this is reasonable and in everyone's interests?' (i.e. mirror their own behaviour)
– 'Why do you think so?'

4. Create 'fog' (non-committal responses and partial agreements), for example:
– 'There is something in what you say. It is an interesting point.'
– 'I understand why you may see it this way. I will think about it.'
– 'We will consider/discuss your point of view.'
– Take the advice given by the Roman philosopher-emperor Marcus Aurelius: 'just do the right thing and the rest does not matter.'

5. Give the responsibility back:
– 'I am sorry you feel that way because my actions have never been designed to make you feel it. I hope you will manage to see and understand this.'

CHAPTER 11

Don't be bullied

We've done it! Another company successfully acquired and integrated. Happy team, happy clients and happy shareholders. All that's left to do is hop on a flight to join them all for the celebration party of the last three years' graft. Back in time for a relaxing family weekend.

At least that's the way it felt as I strolled through Heathrow. I didn't yet know what would be waiting for me a few hours later in Amsterdam.

We'd signed a deal to acquire a fast-growing public relations firm with three European offices. Each office was run by great local entrepreneurs and the whole operation was centralised through the two key shareholders at their headquarters.

Our deal was based on an 'earnout'. Earnouts are a well-known but not universally loved tool for buying service businesses. The final amount paid is a function of the company's profits over a number of years. It's a great way to ensure the continued loyalty and hard work of the founding shareholders because they are incentivised to keep on producing high levels of profit in order to receive their final payout. And it's also a great system for insuring the buyer against inaccurate future profit forecasts from the sellers in industries where a business is often selling intangibles and it is notoriously difficult to make accurate financial forecasts just two or three years out – let alone five years out. With an earnout, everyone's interests – buyer and seller – are, theoretically, aligned. So everybody wins, right?

But the real world isn't lived out in a spreadsheet. People

change. Stuff happens in their private lives. They burn out. They get busy with the next project and stop talking to each other. Clients change personnel, who want new suppliers. Oh, and markets do crazy, unexpected things you could never predict. So, instead of being a godsend, an earnout over several years can often end up being disastrous for sellers. It can feel very isolating and be tough to deliver.

If a deal goes well, both buyer and seller make a lot of money. Sounds like a good thing, right? But getting a life-changing amount of money means that money is no longer a motivating factor for these former entrepreneurs. Instead, they've become rank-and-file employees, but with extraordinary personal wealth. They're right at the pointy top of Maslow's hierarchy of needs pyramid – self-actualisation, where you're more interested in your inner potential and exploring the meaning of life. This makes post-earnout negotiations – where you want to keep the founders involved usefully in the business once they have earnt their millions – a pretty thankless exercise, as your toolkit is almost empty before you even start.

So, back to Amsterdam. Whilst kindly settling the bill for our lovely celebration dinner, the two key sellers – who were based at the Amsterdam headquarters – informed me that they would be leaving the company unless we made it worth their while to stay. Our offer had to recognise their value. If they weren't looked after generously, they would leave the business. They knew we would impose non-compete covenants not to poach the company's staff or clients and they would honour these. But, they went on, the day after those covenants expired they'd open a new office, hire all the best people from the existing firm and take all the clients who remained personally loyal to them.

Suddenly the whole-company 'celebration' meeting that the two of them would be chairing the next morning took on a wildly different complexion. This meeting, it became apparent, was only being put on for my benefit. They'd never previously done anything like it and it wasn't a celebration at all; it was to demonstrate that the business couldn't exist without them.

I cannot recall the price tag they put on the value they believed they brought to the business we now owned. I just remember it was off the charts and had no basis in any recognisably rational model of valuation. This was about ego not valuation. It was about how much they felt we valued both of them *personally*. It was about pride and status and vanity. As the owners, a public company with shareholder responsibilities, we were stuck in a one-way street. Whatever the outcome, there was clearly no way back.

I went back to my hotel room to figure out a response and communicate with my colleagues – the benefit of the Europe-US time zone difference. Our group had just finished the payout for this leading European business. We had to continue to own that business. And we weren't planning on paying for it all over again, as the two founders were effectively asking us to do. Over the years, the founders and I had become close friends. But the path they wanted put the jobs of all their staff at risk and we had to ensure their clients got the service they expected.

This is where personal detachment in any negotiation comes into play. It is a vital skill. We'd built our relationship with the company entirely through the two founders. But, it seemed, the future was going to be without them. So our negotiations were completely focused on securing the office leadership team's commitment to us quickly.

I set out on a road trip to the other offices to build direct relationships with each of their leaders. We'd been told by the two founders that the local office leaders' loyalty was purely to the founders. But our only chance was to appeal directly to them, to elevate their individual status and create a game-changing career and financial opportunity for each of them personally. And the original founders couldn't stop us talking to these leaders of the businesses.

The career element was easy. Dominant founders often have

talented but overshadowed leadership teams underneath them. The second-tier leadership were all very capable. Their issue was lack of experience and drive. The situation we were in as the holding company, and how exposed we were, was no secret. We needed them and we'd have to pay. But the price we'd have to pay was in proportion to the issue rather than completely out of kilter – as it would be if we acquiesced to the founders' effective ransom demand. And, in return, the financial demands that came with the career elevations for this new leadership tier were tough.

We got the leadership team on board and they in turn brought along most of the employees and saved the business. The company never had the same founder-led magic as before; it never could. Nor did it need to. It still did great work, had delighted clients and a happy team producing the results we'd calculated our deal against.

Negotiation lessons

When your counterpart creates what appears to be impossible odds against you, you need to stay objective, be creative and explore your options. Most importantly, you need to revisit your objectives. We needed a successful business. We didn't need the founders. Although it had been the founders who had consistently delivered for us, we had to resist the urge to negotiate with them and, instead, to secure the same outcome by placing our faith in the leadership team directly beneath them. Engaging with those people who had actually delivered the high-quality work and finding a way to recognise their contribution and incentivise their performance outmanoeuvred the party from a seemingly non-negotiable position.

CHAPTER 12

Manipulation will rebound.
Tenderise meat before cooking

As Kirk says, it's a harsh reality that not everyone is well intentioned or ethical. There are people with whom we'd rather not get involved but have no option other than to do so every now and again.

I was advising a US company whose two founders totally relied on each other but single-mindedly focused on their own priorities. In their decade together they'd never socialised with each other – even though they talked together seven days a week. It was strictly business. Each had cultivated their own camp of loyal followers within the company, which created two opposing teams. The company was dysfunctional on so many levels yet was driving sales and profits like nothing I'd previously seen.

Crucially, both founders dealt with their disciples the same way. They both kept their followers starved of praise and hungry for positive endorsement, whilst occasionally berating or ghosting them – often for weeks on end. It felt like a bizarre sociology experiment reminiscent of *Lord of the Flies* – but it worked for the founders and the two camps seemed to know no other way. It was as though they all suffered from Stockholm Syndrome.

These guys were deliberate, calculated and disturbingly cold. In negotiations, they would work on the other party relentlessly to make them so malleable that the founders would get whatever they wanted. It had generally worked.

One individual in the mix particularly stood out. Ian, the head of sales, suddenly stopped getting invited to the daily 5pm drinks at the local bar. This was a crucial part of the company's medieval court ritual; it was where the day's real business was done, in an invitation-only, after-hours cocktail session. Not being there put you on the outside and stripped you of your status, influence and power.

Ian was a strong performer: he had a great flow of new client opportunities, spent six days a week flying around far-flung corners of the USA to convert them, and stayed alongside the delivery team post win to spot incremental opportunities. His flaws? Ambition. Likeability. Success. Ian could potentially generate his own following of disciples – even though he had not consciously sought to do so. For the two founders, such a potential power-threat had to be nipped in the bud. They acted preemptively.

Dis-inviting Ian to drinks was the first tactic and it ramped up fast from there. Employment law on the East Coast of the US bears no resemblance to anything in Europe. Employees are protected from discrimination and being forced to work in a 'hostile workplace', but that's the limit. Next, they removed his share options and cancelled his bonus.

This psychological assault continued for around three months – I observed it on my visits to the office. I asked Ian why he put up with such outrageous BS? He was talented, under-valued and could do so much better. His response was straight and clear. This was all happening because the company was going to be up for sale within the next six months and the founders were going to need a puppet CEO to run the business for them once they'd exited. His calculation was that this was all about getting him softened up for that role – scaring him sufficiently that he would never forget it was their business and he'd be running it for them *regardless* of who owned it.

Time proved him right. The company was sold and he was offered the CEO role on terms that were significantly watered-down relative to Ian's true performance and value to the business.

He'd seen this play out a dozen times with colleagues so the sequence of preceding events hadn't dragged him down; it was the same old dance and he treated it that way. What should have been almost unbearable at a human level – the constant stream of nasty emails, the refusal to talk and the social exclusion – were just steps in the process. He managed to stay above it.

Surprisingly he took the offer without any quibble and the founders celebrated their victory. However, anyone who's ever watched top-level soccer knows that teams are at their most vulnerable just after they've scored. They get caught up in their own triumph and switch off their defences. Exactly the same thing happened to these guys. About six months after the deal went through it was time for the monthly board meeting. The founders made their way in from their respective country retreats. Shortly after the meeting had started, the entire group of a dozen senior managers walked in and presented their resignation letters. If the founders were removed and the CEO fully empowered they would retract their letters. Otherwise the company would be decimated.

The founders had been played at their own game. They'd 'tenderised' their man and got what they wanted with no need for negotiation. But Ian used it to galvanise a full-blown coup that cost them their jobs and the firm they founded.

Negotiation lessons

If you see anyone systematically doing anything 'bad' to other people, know that the time will come when they do it to you. It is purely a question of time. Take a step back and recognise that it is a calculated process; usually it is not emotional or even personal – even if it feels like it is. Plan for it and use your knowledge of their systematic behaviour to your own long-term advantage. You will reap what you sow.

You won't beat the oppressor by confronting them, you have to turn their tactics on them. It is a little like Aikido, the Japanese martial art where the aggressor's own momentum is what takes them down.

PART 3: SUMMARY

In negotiations it is not unusual to be confronted by an aggressive opening position adopted by our counterparts. But what do we do when they won't be reasonable or fair, or, worse still, try to bully you or act in bad faith? As a general rule, you shouldn't allow yourself to be dragged into a mud fight, but in some circumstances it is acceptable to descend to their level.

The complacency of power

First things first, we must aim to cultivate a reputation for fairness. Fairness means that good intentions are rewarded and the relationships we build can flourish.

When the other side uses hardball tactics it usually means that they are more powerful than us or feel they have nothing to lose and are not mandated to move from their position. People who use hardball tactics are unlikely to think and behave in a reasonable manner. It is our job to change their mindset.

When a powerful party perceives no threat from their counterpart, often they will lower their guard. Keep your eyes and ears open for useful information and potential vulnerabilities in their position. Sometimes you need to look outside the negotiation to find your advantage. Can you bring a third party into the equation to shake things up and provide you with leverage?

Fight fire with fire

When you are dealing with bad actors, it is sometimes justified to use power and leverage obtained during the negotiation process to adversely affect the outcome.

When the other party tries to extort, bully or act in bad faith we need a backup plan in order to help the other party to be reasonable, fair and just. By shifting the ground of the debate and taking the initiative, we can restore balance and negotiate, rather than haggle, manipulate and arm wrestle on their terms.

We must always signal that we will work to find an amicable solution; but we will also use our expertise to show that we will exploit any vulnerabilities to force the other party to behave in a reasonable manner if necessary.

Perception is more powerful than reality. A risk presented as a threat is only valid if it is perceived by your opponent as a thing that can cause actual harm to them.

PART 4

Negotiating with Multiple Parties

Negotiating and agreeing is often tough, even between just two parties that know each other very well, if they have slightly different agendas. Even the most loving life partners encounter conflict when one of them has committed to meeting up with friends and the other has promised to help their mother to move into a new home on the same day. With people you know much less well than your spouse – people whose views on the world are dissimilar from yours – you will encounter even greater difficulties.

Making two people agree on something is already a job and a half. What if you have a dozen or more involved? Perhaps they come from different cultures and speak different languages? They will almost certainly have different levels of expertise and different interests. What's the secret to constructing a mutually beneficial multi-party deal?

Imagine you're invited to a farm in southern Italy where they grow some of the juiciest, most succulent, tasty lemons in the world. You are there with your colleagues to negotiate the supply of those lemons for your company as they are a vital ingredient in your bestselling product. You get there, enjoy a tour of the farm and are just about to settle down to negotiate terms over a lovely lunch when you discover there is another party at the table. They are also interested in the lemons and are there to negotiate with the farmer.

What would you do? What was intended to be a straightforward two-party negotiation has just become a multi-party negotiation.

CHAPTER 13

Uniting around a common goal

I was involved in many responses to UK nationals being kidnapped abroad. These jobs involve multiple stakeholders all working together to find a negotiated resolution on behalf of the victims and their families. The majority of these multilateral negotiations take place internally, with our own side.

My unit was contacted by a company whose employees had been taken hostage in a West African country. The company had received very large ransom demands accompanied by threats to harm the victims if the demands were not paid.

The person who received the call from the kidnappers was overwhelmed and needed help. Their insurers had contacted a risk management company who were arranging the deployment of two representatives to manage the crisis in the West African country. We were advised that they would be at the location within two days. In the meantime, we had to engage and manage the local coordinator, who was ill-equipped to deal with this situation.

The coordinator, John, had received calls from the kidnappers, and we gave him advice to help him manage the situation.

The risk management company had advised John not to alert local West African law enforcement, for fear of corruption, as it was essential for them to operate in secret in order to protect the lives of the hostages. We understood the need for secrecy and security, and briefed John on maintaining a firewall between the people already aware of the situation and the outside world.

If there was ever a situation where too many cooks would spoil the broth, this would be it.

Within the team we discussed what the risk management company would be looking for and what they would need. We needed to align our goals. The most obvious common goal would be to save the lives of the hostages – so our every action was focused on that objective. In multi-party negotiations, there are a lot of differences in how everyone sees the desired outcome in detail, so it's necessary to unite the team around one common goal first.

As the frontline contact with the kidnappers, John's lack of training might make matters worse for the hostages. Under considerable pressure and operating in a situation with which he was totally unfamiliar, John might easily say the wrong thing. We told John that his job was to keep the kidnappers calm and not to challenge them in any way which could make them angry. If he made them angry that anger would be redirected at the hostages.

We ran through some role-play calls. One of my team called John and challenged him with the sort of approach we anticipated the kidnappers would use. We helped him create well-worded responses and repeated this process a few times. When the kidnappers called John for real he was able to stay calm and could trot out the prepared answers to the kidnappers' predictable dialogue.

The biggest difficulty we faced was a breakdown in communication. Not the equipment or the phone line but between the people. Imagine the scene: a Nigerian guy shouting at a Scottish guy, both of them speaking heavily accented English and not really able to understand each other. It was potentially a recipe for disaster.

When the risk management operatives arrived in the West African location they would find John better equipped to complement their work. In fact, before their team had even arrived, John had pretty much agreed the conditions of release with the hostage takers.

To this day I am unsure if the risk management contractors knew of our involvement. They didn't need to, and if they had it may have been an unnecessary distraction for them. Working separately and discreetly to prepare John to manage his role in the overall scheme of the crisis better, we helped in the background and the team that had been deployed in-country was able to secure the release of all the hostages.

Experiences like this one prepared me for international negotiations in the corporate world, so when a large Los Angeles-based tech company contacted me to assist with the negotiation and implementation of a contract in two different countries, I was prepared.

The California and London teams seemed to be working in silos and, on a few occasions, had been working directly against each other – to the point where the customer was in danger of cancelling a contract which was worth hundreds of millions of dollars.

Although they were all from the same organisation and shared the same brand, the head of the London group was dealing with the European customers one way and the head of the LA-based group was dealing with their US customers in an entirely different way.

My initial review showed that bosses of equal status in different countries would not be told to fall in line with someone else as they could not see the need to do it any other way. Their way had been successful for them in the past and they had anchored themselves to a position, which dismissed the perspective of their 'opposite number'.

Just the job for a negotiator.

I engaged with both groups separately. I got them to articulate their main objectives, focus on a common shared objective and commit to behaving in a way that would be consistent with that objective. Once that was documented, their commitment had been secured.

We ran a session with both teams where each shared their goals and how they intended to achieve them. There could not have been more synergy if we had tried.

What had been getting in the way was mindset: status, ego, pressure to get an outcome. If we focus on common goals, we become *solution-oriented* rather than combative. It's a bit like the famous example of the British Olympic Men's Rowing Eight squad. For years they had failed to win any medals. Made up of top-class individual athletes, they were pulling in different directions: each individual thought that he, personally, had the key to success and tried to impose his solution on the others. It was only when they shared their common objective – to make the boat go faster – and made that their only criterion for each oarsman's behaviour, technique and commitment, that they started to win gold. Over and over again.

Negotiation lessons

These stories are great examples of where it is sometimes necessary to work in specialist teams towards a common goal to get the best outcome; where separate, specific contributions, all focused towards a common goal, get the job done.

Done badly, this type of working system can lead to problems: the left hand and the right hand don't coordinate, duplication of effort, crossed wires of communication and messy, inefficient and ineffective outcomes.

Done well, this approach is highly effective when it comes to tackling complicated assignments including multi-party negotiations. It works in military operations and generally in crises (including commercial crises). The same happens when you get to a hospital with something serious and urgent – you do your job for the patient, the doctors do theirs, the catering staff theirs, relatives and friends have their own support roles. You take one step at a time and focus on what you can do best. It might diminish your personal scope but it gives you full control and confidence over your field of work.

CHAPTER 14

Simple messages are most persuasive. People agree with what they understand

A digital media company wanted to sell their business. The buyer was from Korea and had never acquired a Western company before. The company consisted of twenty owner-managed businesses scattered over a dozen countries across time zones stretching from São Paulo to Sydney. Each of the twenty owners was a shareholder in their own local company. Each of the businesses was at a different stage of maturity with totally different trajectories and levels of profitability. Some were thriving and would reach top market valuations. Others were performing so poorly it looked like they might have to pay the buyer for the honour of being acquired! All of the involved parties spoke different languages – in both the literal and figurative senses. And for the deal to work, all twenty principals had to agree to sell and to be bought as a single set of shares in a single, controlling entity.

The task seemed enormous. When you see a huge and complicated task in front of you, when the end result looks like 'mission impossible', the most difficult thing is to understand where to start. Even the most brilliant minds get fixated on fiendishly complex, life-changing financial equations and legal scenarios. When you are an expert you tend to quickly jump to the most challenging issues within the area of your expertise. You are focusing on righting the things that seem to you most important and you know for sure they are going to influence the end result. However, in negotiations involving multiple parties, this may simply result in the deal never happening at all.

The negotiations need to be split down into manageable chunks. The first step that needs to happen when you have many people involved in one deal is the same as in any project – you have to unite people around a common goal. If everyone could agree on the principle that this deal needed to happen then we would be just talking about how to get there.

Of course, this is easier said than done. People move quickly beyond the principle to the detail. *How a deal is going to be delivered is intrinsic to getting support for that deal.* A good example of this can be found in the movie *Erin Brockovich*, which is a true story. A legal clerk, Erin, and her boss, Ed Masry, try to get multiple families comprising more than six hundred individuals to sign up to a class action against Pacific Gas & Electric. And they all want to know the details of any deal before signing up to the class action. Erin patiently goes round the loop many times with each family before they are all prepared to sign on the dotted line. You, too, may need to go round the whole loop several times and in several different ways to establish whether there's a deal that can be closed at all.

Sure, the office in Lisbon might be at the start of a four-year explosion in growth, but how much of that growth is attributable to the brand reputation you've already created in New York? And what if the New York business starts to slow down – how will that affect the guys in Lisbon?

As Erin discovered, focusing on all the positive rationale for why a deal should happen sometimes just isn't enough. When someone has their heels firmly dug in, they simply won't listen. At that point the spotlight has to shine onto the consequences of *not* proceeding.

Another important thing to remember in a group deal is that while having to deal with every individual member of the group may demand a lot of resources and effort, you can also benefit from the power of the group. Once you've got someone fully on board, use them to fight your fights for you. Persuasion from within usually changes the dynamics and can dramatically increase the level of trust around the points that need to be agreed. Going back to Erin Brockovich again, she did this brilliantly. She and her boss focused on first signing up those families that *other* families in the community listened to. Once they were signed up, everyone else followed their lead quickly.

Use your allies. Negotiating is a team sport.

Over two weeks we created a series of slightly different versions of the same core structure that could work for our collective group of sellers. Positive progress. But no-one had yet given the slightest thought to whether or not the buyer could stomach what we'd all come up with.

So, from a position where your party is finally all in agreement, you need to turn the deal into something you could sell to the *other* party. This is the moment when you have to be particularly aware of the curse of the expert. The deal may be very complex and have a lot of legal, financial, operational and other commercial nuances. And ideally you need to know and understand them. However, when you have to work out something together as a group you need to be able to *make things sound clear and simple.*

I'm no mathematical genius so I always start by making everything as simple as it can be. I only ever add in any layers of complexity where they're really needed – and in a clear, explicable, staged build. I need such simplicity for myself but I've never worked with anyone who doesn't respond better and faster to this simplification process. This is how our brain works: if we understand something, we tend to believe it.

On this deal, our lawyers' verdict was that they couldn't write it up. They said that the principles were logical but there were too many interconnecting steps – in other words, it was too complicated.

So I created a very simple financial model that could be followed by both sets of lawyers. I boiled it down to just a few key, logically derived numbers that all of the parties could understand. The deal figure simply dropped out at the bottom.

Negotiation lessons

One of my most important mentors was a guy called Richard Mullender who explained to me the concept of implied knowledge.

We worked and taught together all over the UK and abroad. A few years ago, while I was in the Philippines, I expressed some frustration with our students' inability to grasp what was, to me, a relatively simple concept. I asked Richard what he thought was wrong, because we could not seem to get through to them.

As always, his wisdom was unerring. He said that we needed to *simplify* the concepts we were teaching even more because things that were obvious to us were not so obvious to them. He told me that experts should know their topic so well that they can explain it to a child and help them understand it. I accepted that challenge and have been simplifying the concepts ever since.

The more parties, cultures and languages, experts and industries, complexities and nuances you have in your negotiations, the simpler and clearer you have to present it 'in the room'. The more focused and single-minded you have to be at each step. Help people agree step by step. And start by uniting them around common truths, big things and general principles first.

CHAPTER 15

Do not fly solo – find 'insider' support

My client was *the* outstanding business of its type in the UK. It had attracted an overseas buyer with extraordinarily deep pockets that was in a real rush to make something happen. This buyer was itself a pioneering US company operating in the same sector. This was an exciting and high-profile deal to be leading, which would involve some careful navigation. I'd been appointed to advise all the shareholders, so it was crucial to act equally for each individual rather than whoever lobbied hardest and shouted loudest. As in all complex group deal scenarios multiple shareholders had quite different views on the timing, the buyer and the price. I needed help.

A good rule when it comes to such situations is to avoid flying solo. It is critical to capture all the differing perspectives at play and also to interrogate what is being said. In essence there are two roles: listener-in-chief and negotiator. But you also need to have an extra observer, a reliable interpreter of what's going on, ideally somebody on the inside with the full context, knowledge of all of the individuals and the authority to challenge the picture that emerges. Another big role in group negotiations is to act as the representative of all the others with delegated authority. These were the roles I defined for my prospective negotiations partner.

My choice fell on the company's CEO. Phenomenally bright, a great communicator, full of calm confidence and with very high EQ, her ability to work the shareholder base was never in doubt. When selecting your insider ally, these sorts of qualities usually add up to a person who commands the attention of everyone else. Not by being the loudest person in the room or the most charismatic, but, often, being the still, small voice of calm. The person who has the reputation for thoughtfulness, credibility, believability – a track record of displaying integrity and honest dealing. These people may be great on their feet in a group meeting but they might also be quietly spoken, more comfortable – and more effective – speaking quietly in the background to each person individually.

We agreed early on how we'd work together. First of all we needed to ensure that we had the right analysis framework to craft our recommendation. We also agreed that she would deliver that recommendation to her team. The specific pieces of analysis would differ for each individual seller. As would the method of communication to each of them. Going for one all-parties session could have been more time efficient but we decided to have a dozen mini negotiations instead. She knew all the individuals concerned really well, and whilst the set-up was laborious it was tailored and extremely successful.

I sat alongside the CEO for any queries or technical points that came up in the sessions while she delivered the message and secured commitment. This worked for nearly all sellers but there was a hard core of three veteran staffers who we knew would be trickiest. We ran their sessions just as we had with all previous sessions – other than the wrap-up. We didn't try to get commitment from them in the meeting. As we closed with no further questions but no consensus, I left the room and let the CEO conclude the session. She was calm and collected with an air of total authority.

She emerged less than half an hour later. All three signed up. The negotiation had happened while we were all together in the room and she'd not needed to make any concessions or compromises to get their buy-in. She had, however, needed to frame the situation for them and allow them the opportunity to know that they'd been listened to and accommodated as fully as possible. Whilst an independent advisor can become trusted by the team they're advising over a period of weeks, that's nothing relative to the mutual understanding between colleagues that builds over years. She spared me having to get heavy and consequently saved us weeks, which, ultimately, was decisive in closing a deal they all eventually supported.

Negotiation lessons

Decisions nearly always go way beyond the purely rational. You'll rarely be able to unlock most negotiations by using only logical arguments or the size of the cheque – it's usually an appeal to the heart too. And that is better delivered either by a person who's walked in exactly the same shoes or someone who's directly shared the ride to that point. Find that person as your catalyst and ally. They can influence others to line up behind them and build consensus. You don't have to do everything!

CHAPTER 16

Intermediaries: a double-edged sword

Negotiators can sometimes be seen as intermediaries between the decision-makers on each side.

In the world of hostage negotiation, the question always asked about intermediaries is: are they a help or a hindrance?

Intermediaries can take many forms, a trusted friend or relative, a translator or interpreter.

A mutual friend with your opponent may have more loyalty to your opponent, which makes them potentially unreliable. But they can also be useful and connect you with your opponent more closely than you would normally get in critical times of high stress. There are always positives and negatives to everything!

The difference between translators and interpreters is that the latter often provides much-needed context. They can be extremely valuable, but sometimes they can be counterproductive.

I was in a situation where a man was in possession of a gun and allegedly wanted to kill his girlfriend. The situation had escalated from a domestic dispute and the girlfriend had now fled and was hiding in fear. We were told that the man had fired his gun and was now roaming the streets looking for her. We were searching for two people and we had to keep them apart to prevent the man from causing harm to the girlfriend.

As we searched the streets, we were informed that the woman had sought refuge at her mother's address. We went there immediately and removed both of them from the house to prevent them from coming to any harm.

The woman was terrified but was also afraid to cooperate with us for fear that her boyfriend would punish her if she did. Her fear of being beaten told us something: it told us that she did *not* believe the boyfriend would kill her with the gun.

Her perception of his intent was valuable information. We are often faced with treading fine lines of judgement in such a high-stakes role; maintaining a healthy level of scepticism and caution is part of the job. But, whilst we could never let our guard down or simply assume she was right that the boyfriend would not shoot her, it helped us assess the situation differently and open up new possibilities.

After working with her for a while she became cooperative. She showed us images on her phone that he had sent her earlier that day – images of him with a gun. Incredibly, she was able to identify the wallpaper that was in the background of one of the photos as belonging to one of his friends' houses. We now had a likely location for our man.

However, the downside of reassuring her so much and making her feel safe meant that she became emboldened, and during a call with the suspect she began to mock and antagonise him. We were staying in the background as we didn't want him to know we were now controlling events, so we could not censor every word she spoke. And we did not want to end the call as that might arouse his suspicion that she wasn't acting of her own accord. Which would, in turn, cause him to flee the location before we arrived. So we let her carry on.

We arrived at the address in a blizzard of blue flashing lights and stopped in the driveway. To our surprise, we were met by a man who opened the door and welcomed us in. This was unexpected. As the police, we are normally met with verbal insults and requests to see our warrant. Once inside, the situation became clearer, as they directed us to the living room where the body of an elderly woman was lying on the floor. She'd had a cardiac arrest – totally unrelated to the situation we were dealing with (as far as we knew). They thought we were an ambulance crew. Naturally one of the team immediately tried to resuscitate the prostrate woman but was unfortunately too late.

The remaining team members searched the home for the suspect and we found him hiding in an upstairs wardrobe. He did not present any threat to the officers, which was consistent with the earlier assessment by his girlfriend. It was all bravado.

We could not have achieved the arrest without the help of a third party. But third parties always bring a level of uncertainty to negotiations.

In corporate settings, I have found intermediaries to be very valuable, particularly when dealing with people from different cultures.

On one job, an intermediary who was connected to both parties agreed to facilitate the dialogue and keep the process smooth. Things were progressing well: he kept me aligned with the hierarchy at the other end and well briefed on how to behave respectfully with my opposite numbers. It seemed that they had massive respect for one of our major shareholders and naturally we used that to our mutual advantage.

As we neared the end of the negotiations, we shared the term sheet with the intermediary who scanned it for any potential problems. Once the intermediary had passed it, the term sheets would have to be passed by both sides' legal teams – a perfectly normal process.

Much to my surprise, the intermediary called me the following day to tell me that the deal was off. We had enraged the other party by sending the term sheet – they felt they had ownership of this part of the process and had interpreted our proactivity as disrespectful.

My first reaction was to question the intermediary whose sole purpose was to prevent this type of thing from happening. Whilst he accepted his responsibility, he told me that if he was to be blamed for this, his reputation would be forever tarnished in the industry.

Of course, we needed to apologise and explain that we had meant no disrespect. I apportioned no part of the blame to our intermediary and the deal went through the next day.

Negotiation lessons

In a police setting, an intermediary is normally someone between the perpetrator and the police. They could be a lawyer, a family member, a friend. Their role is to help build trust. In a corporate setting, this could be somebody known and respected on both sides of the negotiation.

When you are reaching a critical moment in any negotiation, slow down and make sure your intermediary is well briefed on the approach you wish to take. It is important to prevent behaviour that could destabilise relations and yield negative outcomes. Sometimes, if they don't have skin in the game – if it's not their money, in other words – they don't pay the consequences if it all goes wrong. You will. So make sure you always know what they are doing. An example of this in everyday life is with lawyers in property transactions. By being overly aggressive on behalf of their clients they can cause untold problems and delays where a straightforward conversation between buyer and seller would probably move things along more efficiently and effectively. Keep intermediaries on a tight leash!

CHAPTER 17

Elephants have very long memories

Owning a share entitles the holder to their share of profits and dividends. In most professional services firms the profits generating those shareholder returns come from the company's leadership team. Often the shareholders sit in that team.

The classic employee view of company founders is that they extract too much money from the firm without creating the necessary value. This view builds resentment. And every year, countless startups are founded by disgruntled, disenfranchised senior employees fleeing from such 'unfair' arrangements, intent on righting the wrongs of their former firm and shareholders.

Conversely, the classic entrepreneur view is that employees don't 'get it'. They do not understand that ownership brings with it significant personal risk and sacrifice – starting out in your parents' cold garage or spare room, taking out loans which put your own home in jeopardy, going for years with no income, even risking divorce. Or two divorces. Entrepreneurs reason that they have put in really hard work that employees, even senior ones, never see. They only see the company when it's already a market-leader so they never see or appreciate the hard work that got it there.

In this story, we have a founder who genuinely believed he'd given away all his shares (and hence any value he could get from a sale) to his staff. He felt that his employees neither valued nor appreciated this *largesse* in any way. Conversely, in the other camp, a group of management shareholders felt the founder was holding them back and stifling the business through lack of investment. From their perspective, the founder would get rich off the back of *their* blood, sweat and tears when the sale of the company happened.

Without wishing to give away the punchline, even a simple 'thank you' from the management shareholders to the founder at any point in their dealings with one another would negate the need to write this story at all. Alas, life is rarely that simple. And people are rarely as appreciative as we'd like. (Lest we forget, basic good manners can go a long way.)

But no 'thank yous' were forthcoming. I had to plot a path for both sides to construct a sense of gratitude, or at least respect and acknowledgement, in order to move the negotiation forward. As in most situations where people are afraid of confrontation – with all its potentially catastrophic fallout for the business – intermediaries were appointed. Both the founder and the management shareholder team engaged intermediaries to represent them in this deal. And there was me, negotiating with their negotiators before getting onto the main bout – negotiating with the potential buyer on all their behalf.

We followed good practice and all my negotiating parameters were clear from both shareholder groups. The first consideration was to do with how the sellers would be paid: cash in hand or shares in the acquiring company. If shares, the terms of those shares; the roles for the sellers post deal; plus the normal warranty and indemnity issues. We were aligned on all major points, which was a surprise and substantial relief.

Over the first few weeks we made real progress with the buyer. Even complicated topics of international tax planning went smoothly in a way that seldom happens. Ironically, the fact this was so streamlined created a void on our side. There was no friction or fight with the buyer and we had time and space. Normally time and space are your friend, but in this deal the lack of an opponent created a void. A void that was filled by bringing up all of the resentments that had lain beneath the surface for so long between everyone on our own side.

This was when all the founder's anger about the lack of appreciation shown for the gift of shares came out. It crashed against the team's revulsion at the founder's perceived greed and inflexibility. They felt that he hadn't given the management team a fair slice of the action. If you've previously negotiated through intermediaries, you'll know that they all too often pour high-octane fuel on the flames in any given situation. They don't have 'skin in the game' so can always blame someone else if they don't deliver the deal they promised. It costs them nothing to do so.

I tried to remind both parties that we were supposed to be on the same team against the *real* opponent – our putative buyer. And that, whatever happened, no matter how bitter and unpleasant the tone of our internal negotiations, it was imperative that the buyer never got any sense of our differences. If the buyer sensed there was even a cigarette paper between us, they would play one group against the other to improve their own deal. Even worse, the unedifying sight of our own in-fighting could poison the buyer against the deal itself. This enmity needed to end, and quickly.

The deal with the buyer was doable but we needed catharsis on our side to allow everyone to realise it. I can't claim that I planned a clever route with the founder's advisor; instead it just exploded during yet another call between us. I was being lectured on the management's ingratitude for the umpteenth time. There was no hint of us being able to focus on moving the deal forward. The founder's advisor kept ratcheting up his demands every time he felt the management team's words smacked of ingratitude or weren't contrite enough. He brought in new, wholly ridiculous demands. But this time he pushed it too far. I wouldn't play along with his new demands and refused even to go through the motions of mounting a counter-argument. I had to tell him that I felt his stance was morally outrageous. It went quiet down our phone line for a second or two. Then the tirade began.

I'm not sure how long the stream of invective lasted but it was decisive and cathartic. The advisor knew he'd pushed as far and hard as he could until I'd snapped. He also snapped. We understood each other and he knew he could now go back to the founder and assure him he'd got the best deal he could.

The management team's advisor and I broke down all the component parts to tackle each individual piece of the 'resentment puzzle'. We made some symbolic wins on enough of them to create a sufficient sense of fairness that would allow this group to refocus on life *after* the deal and so move on.

Negotiation lessons

Just like in a road-rage incident, when you're negotiating it's never the specific negotiating point in front of you that you're solving. There's always much more going on in the background or something dredged up from the past. Really you're solving every single piece of accumulated disappointment and bad blood that's been picked up along the way. Sometimes, as in this case, it has built up over years and years. Find the real cause of each party's pain and remove it or parcel it off to limit the damage it can inflict on the main objective.

Remove the whole bee sting to make the pain go away. Don't leave any of it there to keep poisoning everything else.

PART 4: SUMMARY

Negotiations come in all shapes and sizes, but it is rare for it to be as straightforward as a one-on-one discussion. There could be several – even dozens – of stakeholders within your team, multiple parties with whom you must engage, intermediaries, specialists, advisors and decision-makers who are not actively contributing to the negotiation but who have to sign-off on the outcome. All these additional participants add layers of complexity. You must deal with them with skill and dexterity.

Too many cooks

When you see a huge and complicated task in front of you, the most difficult thing is to understand where to start. Often the negotiations need to be split down into manageable chunks and specialist teams must be constructed, whose members can bring their unique expertise to a specific aspect of the negotiation.

But, as we know, too many cooks can spoil the broth. If executed poorly, this type of working system can lead to problems: the left hand and the right hand don't coordinate, there is duplication of effort, crossed wires of communication and messy, inefficient and ineffective outcomes.

When you are negotiating with multiple parties, you must, in effect, negotiate with your own side before you can present a deal to the other party. The most important thing is to make sure you all agree on and unite around a common goal.

Done well, this approach is highly effective when it comes to tackling complicated assignments including multi-party negotiations. You take one step at a time and focus on what you can do best.

You can also benefit from the power of the group. Once you've got someone fully on board, use them to fight your fights for you. Persuasion from within usually changes the dynamics and can dramatically increase the level of trust around the points that need to be agreed. Use your allies. Negotiating is a team sport.

Working with big egos

When you are working with multiple parties who hold powerful roles within their organisations, and who are of equal or similar status, it is likely they will have different opinions about how to achieve your common goal. Their mindset – for instance a preoccupation with status, ego, pressure to achieve an outcome – can get in the way. In these circumstances you must get them to focus on your shared objective and commit to behaving in a way that would be consistent with that objective. If we focus on common goals, we become solution-oriented rather than combative.

Recruit allies

If you are working with people you don't know well, it is useful to have a partner who can act as an extra pair of eyes and reliably interpret the interpersonal dynamics of your team. Ideally they will be somebody on the inside with the full context, knowledge of all of the individuals and the authority to challenge your conclusions.

Look for emotionally intelligent, calm people who are good communicators; not necessarily the loudest or most charismatic voice in the room. They can help break a deadlock by appealing to the better nature of people whom they know and who know and trust them.

Similarly, if you are using an intermediary to negotiate with your counterpart, make sure you appoint someone who is respected on both sides. When you are reaching a critical moment in any negotiation, slow down and make sure your intermediary is well briefed on the approach you wish to take. It is important to prevent language or behaviour that could destabilise relations, undermine your position and yield negative outcomes.

Presenting to the other party

Once your expert teams have come together and you are ready to go to the other party, you need to be able to *make things sound clear and simple*. Do not add layers of complexity. If we understand something, we are more likely to believe it.

The more parties, cultures and languages, experts and industries, complexities and nuances you have in your negotiations, the simpler and clearer you have to present it 'in the room'. The more focused and single-minded you have to be at each step. Help people agree step by step. And start by uniting them around common truths, big things and general principles first.

If there are tensions or unresolved differences within your group, it is imperative that the other party does not become aware of this; present a united, organised front.

PART 5

Tips For Playing Well

Knowing the rules of a game does not mean you will win. As with any game, you learn by playing. So these are some tips, some 'do's and don'ts', things you need to watch out for to enjoy the game and play well.

I was deployed to a report of a man wearing a bomb vest in a restaurant in Glasgow city centre. We had intelligence that he was ex-military and had fired a weapon in England only a few days earlier.

One of the rules drummed into us by psychologists is never to enter into the unreal world of a person with mental illness.

On this occasion, our psychologist advised that if we had any officer with military background, he could pretend to be a commanding officer and as a soldier he would obey his instruction.

So that's exactly what we did. We broke a golden rule that had been followed for a quarter of a century.

To our surprise he marched out of the premises and gave himself up.

CHAPTER 18

The most dangerous time is when you think you're winning

I was contacted by a large business, who asked me to represent them in a resettlement dispute. They had just received an invoice from their American supplier for $45 million, half of the total cost of building a new pharmaceutical plant near Paris. The new factory was a big investment but would reduce transportation costs considerably and provide a long-term advantage for both firms.

Having investigated the costs, my clients told me that this amount was more like the total expenditure for their relocation, not 50 per cent. They felt that their partners were trying to offload all the relocation costs solely onto them. My main client was frustrated:

'How could they do that to us? We've worked with them for years, it's so unfair!'

The client was a philosophical guy. He tasked me with reducing the costs to an acceptable level for them – around $25 million. He informed me that it was normal practice in his industry for larger companies to put their partners under pressure in this way. It helped them to maximise their margins.

To negotiate credibly with the other company, I needed a written mandate from my client so that the other side knew I had the authority to make decisions and had the latitude to look at alternative options. It was important for me to get this agreement so that my status was never undermined; the other side would know from the outset that I would not need to defer to anyone else.

My objective – and reasonable expectation – was to achieve a reduction of around $20 million. In other words, to agree to a deal in the vicinity of $25 million. My walk-away point – the amount at which we were prepared to say 'no deal is better than a bad deal' – was $30 million.

From my experience as a hostage negotiator, I saw the invoice for $45 million as a demand. One which had not yet been accompanied by a threat or a deadline. The absence of a deadline or a threat indicated that I did not have to take that amount too seriously. I commissioned an independent assessment of the costs. This revealed that the amount invoiced was not credible. Establishing the fact that the other side had anchored their price so unrealistically high made it easy to change the momentum in my favour. It is easy to undermine a demand that's based on fantasy, whether it's absurdly high or low.

I advised the other side that they must have made an accounting error. I asked them to re-assess the costs. To help them, I produced my assessment report, which placed the value of the move at $18 million (my anchor). I was not accusatory or confrontational – I needed to give them a graceful way out without losing face. I reminded them that our partnership was long and deep, that it was a relationship of trust built on years of successful transactions between our two firms and that we would not let a simple error affect the trust that had been established over many years. By stating the track record of mutual understanding and respect, I set the tone for the engagement. And once I had established my relationship with the other team's lead negotiator, we were exchanging information at an acceptable level of honesty and transparency.

During the next few negotiation sessions, we ironed out logistics, marketing agreements and common goals. All of these had been conceptually anchored at $18 million, based on the independent assessment I had commissioned, without either of us talking about the final invoice.

The more we discussed the process of relocating, the more I uncovered inconsistencies. When I find similar inconsistencies, I can leverage this knowledge later. I sum up this approach as 'Store it. Don't ignore it!'.

Two weeks later my client took delivery of a new batch of products that had an unacceptably high level of failed samples. This had happened several times before. The opportunity I was waiting for had arrived and my patience was about to pay dividends.

Due to this regular occurrence of quality control failure, I was able to challenge the pricing figures they had calculated and re-anchor them at a much lower and credible cost. I added that the new location would also provide us with an opportunity to review quality control thresholds, stressing the beneficial outcomes for both parties that would come from this. More reliable inventory for us and fewer returns with all the associated transport costs and prompt payment for them.

He accepted responsibility for some issues which lay at their door and told me that he would be prepared to reduce our invoice from the original amount of $45 million to $10 million. I thanked him for his generous gesture, which allowed us to repair some 'broken china' from the past.

My diplomacy had paid off.

I was so pleased with the outcome that I couldn't wait to tell my client about the new offer, which had wildly exceeded our expectations. We had reduced a $45 million invoice to $10 million.

But when my client realised that we had shifted the momentum so drastically, he urged me to push for more. He felt the tide had turned and was still pissed off that the other firm had tried to pull a fast one.

The most dangerous time in any negotiation usually comes when you think you are winning...or have won.

I had forgotten my own teaching! I always talk about the need to anticipate predictable outcomes, one of which is your mandate changing on the whim of a decision-maker.

I was now in a multilateral negotiation – having to negotiate with my own client as well as with the other firm!

I asked the client to trust my judgement. I believed that we had exhausted all options and that we were at the breaking point of our partner's negotiating team. I told him that the cost of finding a new partner and establishing an operating process could take up to 18 months. Delay. Lost supply, lost sales. If we got this wrong we had a lot to lose. I told him that if we pushed for even more discount we were moving from negotiation to gambling and that he personally would likely bear the blame for any losses. I said that I would follow his instructions and seek more concessions if that was what he really wanted me to do. But stressed that this was against my advice and that he was in severe danger of snatching defeat from the jaws of victory.

He relented.

We briefed the lawyers. I had kept them in the loop all through the negotiation. But we needed to ensure that there would be no *re-negotiation* between the legal teams as they set out the minutiae, which would delay an agreement by months. Again, you need to anticipate predictable outcomes, and deals can snag at every stage. Even after the principals have shaken on the deal, the legal agreement and the nature of lawyers trying to make everything watertight can still derail everything.

Negotiation lessons

The most dangerous time in any negotiation is just when you think you are winning. You take your eye off the ball and lose concentration, which leaves an opportunity for the other party to strike.

If you are negotiating on behalf of an organisation, ensure you have a mandate so everyone is crystal clear about (a) what you are aiming to achieve and (b) your authority to strike a deal without recourse to higher authority. Nothing is more undermining than having to defer to another in the middle of negotiations.

Anticipate the knowns and try to anticipate the unknowns but probables.

Store information, don't ignore it (or use it piecemeal). Package it all up together and then use it so it has much greater impact.

Stay positive and diplomatic always – unless losing your temper is a deliberate tactic, as we'll see in the next story...

CHAPTER 19

Shout and sometimes you'll be heard

Negotiating styles can vary greatly from one culture to another and they don't always follow the obvious cultural stereotypes you might expect. When you're at an impasse in a highly structured negotiation, sometimes the best way to break it is to deliberately invoke emotion. Sometimes emotion unintentionally comes to the fore and has the same positive disruptive effect. If an escalation is needed to push through, emotion is a tool to consider.

We were acquiring a business in Germany. I'd like to claim that my use of emotion was a personal masterstroke, but, in truth, it was done unintentionally in a moment of sheer panic.

We'd been working on the acquisition for about six months. The principal seller had spent a lifetime negotiating sports sponsorship deals for major soccer teams so he was a tough, uncompromising character and a seasoned dealmaker. Our due diligence was telling us that we needed to take another look at some of the commercial terms of the deal – 'deal speak' for reducing the price. We felt some of the deals the company had with sports bodies weren't everything they could be, and this needed to be reflected in the final price. People don't tend to like it when you reduce the price. And it's not a pleasant experience to negotiate down if you haven't used due diligence in an intentional manner.

It's common for people to seek their own personality traits in their advisors. Often in a more exaggerated form. The principal seller had hired an especially formal and intransigent advisor whose view was that a deal's a deal, so we just needed to get on and do it or not do it. He wouldn't listen to objective reasoning or any amount of corroborative analysis. We tried side channels and picked off more sympathetic individuals on the sell-side to raise the issues from the inside. All to no effect. We had exhausted the normal toolkit. We were all pretty frustrated and I was personally exhausted by it all. The final straw was an email from the seller late on a Friday afternoon effectively giving us an ultimatum.

I forwarded the email to our team with a pretty frank assessment of how I felt about the situation and my views about the seller and his advisor. It was expletive-heavy – not the most professional communiqué I've written – but I was confident that my mood and opinion reflected my wider team's experience, so I shut the laptop and headed to grab a much-deserved early evening beer.

As soon as I shut the lid I realised what I'd done. Left arrow to forward and right arrow to reply-all. I had pressed the right arrow. Aaaagh! Our IT department had gone home for the weekend and the email was out there in the ether just waiting to explode on arrival. Nearly nine months invested in buying the best-in-class business in a highly strategic geographic market and hundreds of thousands of euros sunk in professional fees. Surely this was a sackable offence? And getting fired would be nothing compared to the ear-bashing I'd get from the seller when he opened his inbox.

My mobile rang a couple of hours later. It was the seller. I steeled myself for crucifixion. He was calm and positive. He agreed with me. He was all the things I'd called him – absolutely right – and he was ready to move forward with our proposal as he could see that he'd pushed us as far as we could go. No hard feelings and let's finish the deal off quickly from here.

I put the phone down. More in relief than elation. That hadn't been what I expected at all. With hindsight I could see that my uncontrolled outburst was something the sellers had intentionally sought to provoke. I'd seen it play out a couple of weeks previously in a different context and just hadn't joined the dots.

The company had a non-executive director who'd been tasked with unblocking a problem with one of the seller's employment contracts that was holding up closing the deal. The non-exec and I had debated how we'd do this as we had no real leverage and the seller was holding out for an inflated title and salary. He was ultimately in a replaceable role but it would have caused a lot of immediate post-deal bad feeling amongst staff that would have stuck to us as buyers and tarnished our overall working relationship with our new partners. So we agreed to his request for the new title and some, but not all, of the money. He still wasn't budging despite being face to face with us – where we might have expected him to succumb to the pressure.

The non-exec took me to one side and said he wanted ten minutes on his own with this guy to talk to him in his native tongue. The non-exec's assessment was that this was a man convinced that he could only win and had lost sight of what he might have to lose. It sounded like a reasonable tactic to persuade him to concede on these final points, but I hadn't anticipated how the non-exec would deliver the message.

I sat in an office opposite the boardroom and within a minute there was shouting of the volume you'd hear in the home fans stand at a football game where the referee has just allowed a penalty against the host side in the last minute of extra time. It was noisy. And it went on and on. This language isn't one in my repertoire, but the volume and tone made that irrelevant. About ten minutes on, the non-exec emerged and the job was done. What had he done to get this result? He'd asked the guy in exceptionally colourful terms how his wife would feel about him coming home without the money from the deal, without a job and with his career in tatters? Although I'd never found the shouty locker-room technique effective, this seller had witnessed an ordinarily logical and very reasonable individual totally lose it. This immediately convinced him that he had indeed pushed the boundaries of the negotiation as far as humanly possible and we were at breaking point. So he'd relented, satisfied he'd got the best he could and all was now good. We all shook hands and went back to our desks as if we'd all just had a very civilised afternoon together.

Negotiation lessons

Don't hold back on the use of emotion out of concern that it might jeopardise a negotiation built on logic and persuasion. It won't. It might just lift people out of the realm of the rational to be able to settle back into the negotiation with a new perspective.

CHAPTER 20

Playing spoof for $50m

Lots of negotiation is deeply technical. Based on analysis, logic and reasonable arguments. The best negotiators, however, are sufficiently detached from the details to have a view on the process *as a whole* and how to keep it moving on the right path. Even if that means re-drawing the map multiple times along the way.

We'd been running the negotiation process for nearly two months. Each concession was getting progressively smaller and we were inching along with almost no momentum. The gap was a sizeable $50 million.

Fatigue and frustration are killers in protracted negotiations. They drain creativity, erode trust and allow the mind to start playing tricks on you. To create its own fictional issues that start seeping into the real negotiation. We'd definitely reached this point and it was time to force a conclusion.

Our heads were all too much in the spreadsheets. We'd done all manner of financial scenario modelling. We'd conceived all kinds of increasingly convoluted deal structures to deliver the target returns in different ways for different growth and profitability scenarios. And we'd started writing long, complicated sentences like that last one. It had all become too hard, too complicated and too theoretical. On paper the deal worked beautifully. In practice it was undeliverable. We needed something simpler.

We could see that our team was rapidly running out of gas and needed something to radically shake it up. But we needed to ensure that our shake-up didn't backfire on us and do irreparable damage to the deal.

Someone suggested we should just play spoof for it. Yes, you read that right: spoof – the game often used to settle who will pay a restaurant tab. Players are given the same number of coins each. Each player places their coins in a clenched fist, so no one can see how many coins each player has. They could hold none of the coins, all of them or any amount in between. All the players hold out their clenched fists and take it in turn to call how many coins in total they think are being held collectively in the clenched fists around the table. Each round, the person who guesses the total number of coins being held wins and is out. The other players play another round. The loser is the one who fails to guess the correct number of coins between the last two players left in the game. They pay the bill.

It was a throw-away comment. Everyone laughed. It was plain ludicrous. We get back to the serious business of coming up with something plausible. But the suggestion of playing spoof stuck.

Our buyer was totally seduced by the company's A-List clients and the work it did for a high-profile NFL team. We'd all been around the negotiating table for way too long and had gone number blind. We ditched the lawyers' offices for our directors' box at the stadium and a Sunday-night game. We'd make our box the negotiating room and we'd stack it with our most evangelistic A-list clients to impress the buyer. This gave us the home-team advantage, but that wasn't enough. We needed something that told them we were really serious about our demands and showed them why they should listen.

So how does spoofing fit into this? I wasn't the mastermind of this idea, but I sold it to myself as pure theatre – a way to make an important point. I was slightly worried that it might backfire and make the buyer think our two key shareholders were nuts. But I persuaded myself that we'd got to know each other well enough that they'd probably just see it as a bit of fun. But as far as the two sellers were concerned, this was serious. They really were prepared to spoof for $50m!

We got to the box early. On a little table by the door was a bag. In the bag were two replica shirts for the football team. One had $175m printed on the reverse and the other $125m. The two acquisition prices in play – a $50 million difference between the two. You couldn't see into the bag, only put your hand in and pull out a shirt. Simple: the buyer picks out a shirt from the bag and whichever it is will be the price they pay for the business.

The stadium started to fill and so did the box. Only the three of us were in the know, while the rest of the cast started getting ready for the game with some beers and snacks. I certainly had no appetite and, although they were doing a good job hiding it, I knew the others were stressed too.

The three representatives from the buyer finally showed up just as the game was starting. Little did they know that they were about to get ambushed in the most spectacular way.

I'll never forget the look of sheer unbridled terror on the faces of the investors, imagining themselves having to explain to their shareholders why the deal had cost $50m more than they'd agreed. My clients knew this wasn't the kind of panic that meant they'd won. It meant the deal was about to disappear in a puff of smoke. They immediately burst into hysterical laughter, lots of back-slapping and 'we had you there'.

In the car back into the city at the end of the game it was deathly quiet. We all travelled back together. I don't think any of them could process what had really happened.

Where did we end up? As always in negotiations nobody *won*. We all came out of it okay. They got the point that $175m was the magic number and showed us a way that if we hit achievable targets within a short period of time they'd more than happily pay. If.

Negotiation lessons

Sometimes you have to just go with it. In fencing, boxing and martial arts, the feint is a deadly weapon. This kind of feint was seismic but it was proportional to the gulf that had to be bridged. It jolted us all out of stasis and forced a total reset, finally allowing a good deal to get done. If you're in a stalemate, try something lateral.

CHAPTER 21

Being torpedoed by your own side

Sometimes all the stars align. You figure out a compelling strategic fit between one company (the buyer) and another (the seller). Both companies already know each other, trust one another and have admired each other for years. The personal chemistry is great. All this should make for the simplest negotiation in history.

The buyer's CEO is one of the best-known business leaders in the industry – hugely intelligent, experienced, highly principled, straightforward and true to his word. Not a detail person but happy to rely on a small group of long-standing advisors to deliver the precise terms in the way that he wants. He'll breeze into the closing meeting for the signing.

His counterpart, the key shareholder, founder and CEO of the company that is selling, is equally straightforward. No nonsense. This is the first time he's been involved in the sale of a business. So he's feeling his way, piecing together the doubtless invaluable advice he's been offered by friends all through the process.

Everything is well set-up. Miraculously, it then gets even easier; the buyer is serious about this purchase so the first offer is very good. Ordinarily this becomes a question of closing as quickly as possible to prevent anyone interfering, overcomplicating or otherwise spoiling a near-perfect deal. However, the lack of any friction unsettles the seller. His friends tell him that he must be under-selling. To counter these ill-informed, gossiping mates we put him in touch with a couple of highly experienced, impartial advisors who reassure him that the deal on the table really is excellent. They advise him to agree and close out the deal. But the whispering friends' warnings have penetrated deep inside him and he just won't be satisfied without testing them personally.

How do we manage our client's forthrightness? He believed that 'if you don't ask, you don't get'. He was determined to ask. In the other corner we had a buyer who made it an article of faith to table exactly the right offer, first time, every time. Who had built his reputation as an acquirer of companies around this principle and who walked away if his spirit of fairness was not reflected in the seller's response.

True to form, the buyer had framed the key terms and left a lot of discretion to his advisory group to resolve everything else. The buyer's lead negotiator had a simple and short list of immovable points. One non-negotiable was that this was a 10x earnings deal. Maximum.

Acting for the seller, I scrutinised all the analysis. The 10x multiple was clearly a critical red line and the buyer would not go any higher. But there were plenty of other opportunities we could combine into a package that would be open to discussion. Enough to merit my confidence that my client wouldn't feel the need to negotiate himself. Which, I knew, would put the whole deal at risk.

Without doubt, keeping the buyer's CEO and my client out of any direct negotiations was key. They needed to focus on the relationship and the strategy. What we hadn't counted on was the two principals having lunch together that day.

I knew the lunch was in the diary and my client – the seller – had told me that he wanted to make one request of the buyer and to make it in person. It was a point that was already on the shopping list that I knew was going to be acceptable so it seemed harmless to acquiesce.

I was slightly surprised to see my counterpart negotiator's phone number come up on my screen in the middle of that afternoon. Perhaps my client went directly to another meeting after lunch – it would have been good to have had a debrief, just as a courtesy, before I picked up the negotiation again. Still, I knew that over lunch they had only been talking about an innocuous point, so I took the call without any trepidation. Oh dear. Not what I'd expected. My counterpart blew a gasket. Apparently, my client had announced over lunch that whilst he was happy with the rest of the deal, he felt that a 12x multiple would be a lot better than a 10x multiple. Having dropped this bombshell, he'd then continued eating his lunch and waited for a response. The buyer could have walked away from the table and the deal at this point. Uncharacteristically, he acquiesced to my client's request – but briefed his team to extract a balancing package to compensate for the increased cost of acquisition.

The compensating package of demands was severe. As was the fallout.

My client's behaviour at the lunch prompted hard questions about whether he really was the kind of guy the buyers thought he was. At this point I'd not even had the chance to speak to my client and the deal was in serious jeopardy. It was clear that I had to save my client's reputation or lose the deal. I needed to fall on my sword. I did. I made out that the lunch request had been part of a deliberate plan that I'd hatched. In other words, it was all my idea – my client was innocent and undeserving of any suspicion attached to the conversation. This 'admission' would cost me dearly in the future with the buyer's organisation but at least restored the perception of my client's integrity in the eyes of the buyer team. Sometimes an own goal, it seems, can save the match.

I took the rocketing, offered up the full suite of concessions and graciously accepted the extra two points on the multiple.

Negotiation lessons

Persuading someone who has never previously been through a negotiation that they've got it easy is an almost impossible task – they just don't have the reference framework to know when they're staring a gift horse in the mouth. They have created assumptions and allowed others to implant the idea that the other party has bad intent. Go with it. Recognise that no matter how good the opening offer, you're going to need to deliver a little more and assume that the other side has factored this in no matter how much they protest to the contrary.

CHAPTER 22

Bluffing or for real?

This story is about when we think the other side is bluffing and get it wrong. We get it wrong because we apply our logic and context to the situation and not theirs. It is also a slightly different take on high-stakes negotiation. Sometimes, a negotiation is actually a cover for something else. In situations where there is extreme hazard to life and limb, it is the negotiator's job to keep the other party talking whilst a different operation altogether is going on simultaneously. This was the case with the Iranian Embassy in the London siege of 1980. Negotiations were taking place when the SAS stormed the embassy to release the 26 hostages.

How can we tell when the other side is bluffing? In games of poker they always talk about 'the Tell' – a noticeable tic or a change in behaviour which gives away the player's mental anxiety or excitement about their hand and thus betrays their situation.

Whilst kinesics – reading body language – can be useful, it isn't 100 per cent reliable. Without the context another person brings with them, assessment of their body language happens in a vacuum and is, therefore, meaningless. For example, a person in an arms crossed stance conventionally means that they are closed and defensive. But for many people, crossing their arms feels comfortable and helps them to feel relaxed. As in so many other areas of negotiation, jumping to conclusions can be flawed.

In a game of poker, it can be the difference between winning and losing.

As a hostage negotiator, when a person is standing on the edge of a bridge, I cannot afford to get it wrong. It can be the difference between life or death.

When going through initial training, I remember the words of my inspirational course director, telling us that soon we would have 'life in the palm of your hands'. It was a sobering thought and one that separated those who were there for the right reasons and those who thought it would be a nice course to attend.

Even back then, some of my colleagues would say things like, 'If they were really serious, they would have jumped.'

This was certainly not the opinion of the experienced hostage negotiators who came back to the training course to share their stories of things they had faced.

On my very first job, I attended the Erskine Bridge, a few miles from Glasgow, and was confronted by a female standing on the wrong side of the barrier. It was a cold, wet, dark, windy evening and I was not comfortable approaching her.

Ahead of me was an experienced negotiator who had decided to react to her imminent threats and withdraw temporarily and give her some space. He told me that he thought she was deadly serious. I remember him telling me, 'she threatened to jump if I did not get back, I don't think she's bluffing'.

With a healthy scepticism, I continued forward slowly and with each step I received some discouraging words. Her anger towards a stranger told me that something was burning inside her.

Despite the threats, I confronted her with the finality of her intended actions. We are often told that suicide is a permanent solution to a temporary problem. Within that explanation, I told her that I saw the ending to a life which had great potential and I actually used the phrase 'What a waste of such a beautiful woman this will be'.

She turned around and looked straight at me. I had been told that this is an indicator that the person is ready to jump. I had seen videos so many times of a calmness coming over people just before they commit to their final act.

She told me that she had never been told that she was beautiful by any other man than her dad. He had died many years before. I had found a connection with her.

If you think that is the end of the story you could not be more wrong.

My flattery was something that she liked to hear. I recognised the impact and, given the context, neither of us interpreted it as a flirtation tactic. But it did change the conversation style, at least for some barriers to come down.

After a period of talking to her, I realised that she intended to die, but had just not yet worked up the courage to jump.

She was standing on the wrong side of the barrier, which was about five feet high. She had climbed over quite an obstacle to get into that position. Facing outwards with only her heels balancing on the ledge, she was swaying in the wind. She had already taken her ability to balance to extreme levels as the arch and ball of her feet were resting on nothing at all.

In that moment, I began to fear the 50-foot drop to the water below. My leg was shaking whilst I was trying to think of things to say that would make her change her mind. If she would even just take hold of the railings, I would feel better. How ironic. I was there to make her feel better not the other way around.

I told her I could not hear her clearly because of the howling wind gusting across the bridge. As her trust in me became stronger, she allowed me to come closer.

I realised that she was hoping that mother nature would take her life, but instead human nature took over. I broke the rules of hostage negotiation and grabbed her firmly and would not let go.

She started screaming and shouting and pushed against the railings trying to break my grip on her. There could only be one outcome.

I screamed for help and, very quickly, I was joined by a colleague and three fire and rescue officers who were at the scene. Between the five of us, we managed to hold onto her despite a violent struggle to bring her back over the barrier.

Her fight was so determined that I knew she did not want to live. To think some people on the course had branded such behaviour attention seeking! Nothing could have been further from the truth. I knew then that I needed to find a method of evaluating a person's true intent in such situations and change the way we dealt with them.

Negotiation lessons

Before this incident, I could not imagine anyone really wanting to end their life, but when I realised they wanted to end their pain, I began to understand the self-destruct signals. If we cannot offer hope of a good future, our counterparts will often be prepared to cause themselves harm.

After that incident, I looked at behaviour assessment in a completely different way and shared my story with other students. Superficial assessments of people and circumstances will never be enough when we are dealing with matters of life and death. I would not allow anyone to become complacent in their approach to such situations. And, having broken the rules on physically intervening, I had to replace that with a better and more intelligent response.

When we are responsible for the safety of others, the stakes are too high to gamble. When we truly take time to listen to other people and validate their feelings by showing empathy, they are more likely to feel heard and understood. Only once you have understood the context of *their* perspective will you be able to present logical solutions.

Anything else is just an exchange of views without any real connection.

PART 5: SUMMARY

If the other side has anchored their asking price unrealistically high, you will be able to change the momentum in your favour. It is easy to undermine a demand that's based on fantasy. Ensure you are not accusatory or confrontational – you need to allow them a way to climb down without losing face.

Store information and wait for the moment of maximum impact to utilise it. Don't ignore useful information or use it piecemeal. It's the same with concessions: don't leak them one at a time; package them into a compelling offer instead. If you leak information or concessions you lose the collective power they have to generate reappraisal by the other side and so shift the momentum of your dialogue.

Positivity, sensitivity and diplomacy are the best options under most circumstances, but sometimes losing your temper is a useful tactic to deploy. Sometimes the best way to break an impasse is to utilise raw emotion.

The most dangerous time in any negotiation usually comes when you think you are winning. Just because the finish line is in sight, don't lose concentration or get complacent.

If you are negotiating on behalf of a third party, ensure you have a mandate to speak for them so all parties are clear about what you are aiming to achieve and your authority to strike a deal.

To return to the very first lesson we shared, remember that empathy is the foundation of every successful negotiation. Listen to other people, validate their feelings by showing empathy, make them feel heard and understood. You won't be able to present logical solutions until you have understood the context of their perspective.

Conclusion

Our brains love to simplify everything and replace more difficult questions and situations with simpler ones. Why? Because our brains like to save energy and simpler questions have simpler and more straightforward answers. We set out to write a book that was as free as possible from jargon and which doesn't pretend that if you follow a set of prescribed rules, negotiation will be easy and effortless. It will never be. As we said right at the start, negotiation is nuanced.

Most people mistake bargaining – haggling – for negotiating. Bargaining is just the simplest form of negotiation, so our 'lazy' brains default to it and this is as far as most people's understanding of negotiation goes. For most people in business, for example, this means we default to thinking it's all about the money ('sharpening your pencil' as it's called) – haggling over the sum that you are willing to accept and the client is willing to pay. If you realise you are being drawn into haggling, your choice is either to say 'yes' to it and haggle – you will end up with the worse end of the bargain because they will dictate the terms – or to try and steer communication with your counterpart out of the haggling mode and back into proper negotiation, which involves a lot more than just the price of something.

Having a proper negotiation conversation means you talk about mutual objectives and a partnership of mutual benefit in terms other than pure money.

Which is why we opted to share real-life stories in plain language which illustrate how you do that *in practice*. Stories which will equip you with *perspicacity*: the ability to apply clarity, insight and discernment in different situations. To take nothing for granted; to ask better questions; to remain alert to clues; to be able to use your internal radar better and, ultimately, to work out *what's really going on* so you negotiate from a position of strength. Whatever the situation.

Finally

If we boil everything down, what key lessons can we draw from all our stories?

1. It's a game.

If you think about negotiation as a game you will enjoy it much more. Do not dread the possibility of a loss – that will cramp you up. Instead, learn how to play (this book will help), practise and start enjoying it. You cannot win any game if you do not like it.

2. It takes two to tango.

You cannot control others. But you can learn to control yourself. This is a very powerful skill and the bedrock of staying composed, alert and immune to manipulation and other tricks people employ. When the other party tries to extort, bully or act in bad faith, you need a back-up plan in order to help the other party to be reasonable, fair and just. By shifting the ground of the debate and taking the initiative, we can restore balance and negotiate, rather than haggle, manipulate and arm wrestle on their terms.

3. It is all about relationships.

Any partnership is first of all a relationship. Whether it is relatively short, simple and transactional – just for the duration of the negotiation, as with some of Kirk's police stories – or long-lasting, complex and multi-faceted, as is often the case in business dealings, they are all about relationships. The relationship you have with yourself and the relationships you have with others. And healthy relationships are not about winning and losing.

4. You don't have to know the answer in advance to every problem that you're going to face. But you do need to be properly prepared. But you will find a path through by staying focused on your own definition of your 'win', being alert to the other party's behaviour and by remaining dispassionately connected with them. As with any athlete playing a game, you need to prepare thoroughly for the match, be highly aware of what's going on around you when engaged with the other side, and stay on the balls of your feet so you can move in any direction with ease – whichever way the game turns. The more flexible and adaptable you are, the quicker and more agile you can be when something you weren't expecting happens.

Negotiation is a fascinating subject and we are lucky to have made it our life's study and the mainstay of our careers. Negotiating may never be your favourite thing to do, but hopefully it will be much less stressful than it was when you started to read this book. Apply the lessons from the stories and you will achieve better outcomes from the negotiations you have – in business and in home life. Because now you'll be negotiating more like a pro.

Glossary of terms

Anchored position

The opening/first offer made by either party in the negotiation.

Bad faith actors

People whose intent is not to work constructively to deliver the normal aims of a negotiation (see definition below), but instead to frustrate, disrupt or do harm to achieve their goals.

CFO

Chief Financial Officer

Due diligence

The process by which an acquirer satisfies its enquiries to ensure that the asset (house, car, company, etc) it is buying is as the seller has represented it during the sale process.

Earnout

A method of acquiring a business where the price paid isn't set at the moment of sale. Instead, the parties agree a pricing formula based on future performance or events that will ultimately determine the price, with only a down payment being made at the point the sale is completed.

Intellectual property

An invention, a logo, a story, a work of art created by the mind which has value and is owned by the party who created it or by the entity which bought it legally.

Loan note

A form of debt between a buyer and seller. Typically a simple contractual promise to pay a specified amount on a future date, potentially interest bearing and secured against company assets of the buyer.

Multiple

Transaction multiples are a financial metric used to value a company. While asset-heavy businesses might be valued based on the physical assets themselves, services businesses typically are not. Instead, they tend to be valued on a multiple of their revenues or profits.

Negotiation

A way to obtain an agreement in a situation of expressed disagreement, opposing different stakes, between two or several parties, so that each party obtains what is fair to them. Alternatively, the process of bringing together two or more parties who are apart to a mutually acceptable outcome.

Non-executive director

An individual retained by a company to provide independent and objective advice, usually based on their industry experience or technical expertise. The role has no executive responsibility and is purely advisory. It has no legal power as a director does.

Party

An individual, group of individuals or organisation participating in a process of negotiation.

Principals

Within a negotiation there will often be many professional advisors and other protagonists. Their role is to advise and guide the principals – those directly benefiting or suffering from the outcome of the negotiation – but they are not part of the negotiated outcome.

Shareholder

The holder of a share in a company with associated benefits of ownership of the entity.

Acknowledgements

Jim Houghton:

The list is long and wide, but Noel Penrose, Michael Birkin and Dale Adams gave me my big break and were fabulous role models to attempt to follow. I'm still trying. Graham Beckett will always be my yardstick as an M&A advisor, and every time I work with Jo Evans or Tim Birt I learn from them and feel like a better human being for the experience. Of course my greatest thanks go to all my M&A clients over the years who've trusted me with their life's work.

Kirk Kinnell:

I have been fortunate to have so many great people around me for a long time that there are literally too many to mention. I do not mean that as an insincere platitude but as a genuine expression of gratitude for so many people in the world of law enforcement and hostage negotiation who sacrificed their time and expertise for the benefit of others.

Index